GOD AS OTHERWISE THAN BEING

Northwestern University
Studies in Phenomenology
and
Existential Philosophy

GOD AS OTHERWISE THAN BEING

Toward a Semantics of the Gift

Calvin O. Schrag

Northwestern University Press
Evanston, Illinois

Northwestern University Press
Evanston, Illinois 60208-4210

Copyright © 2002 by Northwestern University Press.
Published 2002. All rights reserved.

Printed in the United States of America

10 9 8 7 6 5 4 3 2 1

ISBN 0-8101-1922-6 (cloth)
ISBN 0-8101-1923-4 (paper)

Library of Congress Cataloging-in-Publication Data

Schrag, Calvin O.
    God as otherwise than being : toward a semantics of the gift / Calvin O. Schrag.
        p. cm.—(Northwestern University studies in phenomenology & existential philosophy)
    Includes bibliographical references and index.
    ISBN 0-8101-1922-6 (alk. paper)—ISBN 0-8101-1923-4 (pbk. : alk. paper)
    1. God. 2. Ontology. 3. Postmodernism. I. Title. II. Series.
BT103 .S37 2002
211—dc21   2002002168

To my granddaughter
Jessica Marie Stampfl
A gift for us all

Contents

Preface

There are always multiple factors that motivate an author to write a book. A reader may well expect to be informed about some of these at the outset. An appropriate place to do this is in the preface. Although academic protocol would have all explanations of the text remain internal to the projected arguments and analyses, it is difficult for authors to avoid autobiographical reminiscences in giving an account of the motives that animate their works. Authors cannot so easily shed the formative influences that have contributed to the designs of their historically situated projects. And when an author has published previous works, some account of the relevance of these, either in the way of continuity or discontinuity, would help contextualize a current endeavor.

Although there are no clearly definable heroes in the story I tell in the following pages, there are numerous interlocutors. Many of these interlocutors, given the fragility of a finite memory, will regrettably remain unnamed. Among the interlocutors are previous mentors of mine, past and present collegial associates, including students from the beginning of my career to the present. These mentors and colleagues have in different ways helped define the topic and the format of this particular work. The topic, which is basically an inquiry into the concept of God, is a relatively new topic in my writings. However, an interest in the topic extends all the way back to the days of my graduate studies during the middle 1950s. The director of my doctoral program, John Wild, and another influential member of the Harvard faculty who served on my committee, Paul Tillich, were my principal mentors for the dissertation exercise. The one was a philosopher with strong theological interests; the other was a theologian with strong philosophical interests. From the combined influence of these two mentors there resulted a confluence of philosophical and theological ideas that was destined to leave a permanent deposit in my own professional development.

It was also at this time that I had the opportunity to meet a young fellow graduate student, an exchange student from Paris, who subsequently achieved some prominence, both in his native France and in other parts of the world. This fellow graduate student was Jacques Derrida. I have followed his illustrious career during the past decades with respectful critical interest. His writings have been a catalyst in my own thinking, which at times has developed *with* them and at other times has reacted *against* them. In the text that follows, the impact of a critical exchange with Derrida's extensive legacy in philosophical and religious thought will at times become noticeable.

A year of study abroad, thanks to the resources of the Fulbright Scholar Exchange Program, took me to Heidelberg University, where the tutelage of Karl Löwith and Hans-Georg Gadamer contributed in no small manner to my dissertation research. In the fifties there was much ado about existentialism at European universities, particularly at Heidelberg, where numerous courses and seminars on Kierkegaard, Sartre, and Jaspers were being offered. I noticed that the name of Heidegger, however, was somehow conspicuously absent from the course listings. This I found somewhat puzzling, but I was soon to learn that *all* of the courses were on Heidegger! In a seminar on Kant's *Critique of Pure Reason*, for example, the progress in the rigorous examination of the text was at times inhibited, but also at times facilitated, because of a proclivity on the part of the professor and students alike to make running comparisons with the texts of Heidegger!

Returning to Harvard for the completion of my graduate studies, I finished and submitted a dissertation on Kierkegaard and Heidegger, which later was readied for publication as my first book, *Existence and Freedom: Towards an Ontology of Human Finitude* (1961). It should come as no surprise that it is difficult to write about Kierkegaard and Heidegger without having philosophical and religious topics and themes crisscross at rather crucial junctures. Thus in this very early work certain background interests that circumscribe the current project are already discernible.

The formative influences of early mentors, past and present colleagues, and the never-ending procession of students, always need to be coupled with the conditioning factors operative in the philosophical movements and trends of the day. Philosophizing does not take place in a cultural and historical vacuum. To philosophize is to respond to that which particular philosophers, past and present, have thought and said and written. With the appropriate apologies to John Donne, let me submit that no philosopher is an island entire, cut off from the mainland of the philosophical republic. One's philosophical odyssey as an author thus requires that one take an inventory of the times and respond to the occurrent beliefs and practices in a discerning manner. In exploring the contributions of nineteenth- and twentieth-century European thought, it became necessary for me to respond in my various writings to the developments of existentialism, phenomenology, hermeneutics, critical theory, and structuralism—all of which helped shape the contours of continental philosophy during the twentieth century.

As is well known not only in philosophical circles but also within the wider public postmodernism has of late been very much in the philosophical news. The reports by the various commentators on the scene are not always in accord with each other. Much depends on the particular site on which postmodernism is practiced. It appears to make some difference whether one does postmodernism in departments of philosophy, theology, literature, communication, gender studies, or the several social sciences. Each of these disciplines fashions a somewhat different take on the phenomenon, all of which is an indication of what may be a centralizing thematic that runs through the movement—namely a bold and aggressive overture toward pluralism and heterogeneity, a pluralism of modes of thought and social practices and a heterogeneity of language games.

It is thus of some importance that authors make as clear as possible at the outset the vantage point from which they proceed. Such would seem to be particularly the case when postmodernism is under discussion. My exploration of this somewhat rugged terrain was already undertaken in two previous works, *The Resources of Rationality: A Response to the Postmodern Challenge* (1992) and *The Self after Postmodernity* (1997). In my researches on the topic I found recurring references to the alleged founders of postmodern thought (chiefly Nietzsche and Heidegger in Germany and Foucault, Derrida, and Lyotard in France), which were coupled with reiterations of the solemn pronouncements of the "death of God" and the "death of Man." It was Nietzsche, of course, who brought the death of God theme into prominence; and it was Foucault who some decades after Nietzsche called the world's attention to the death of Man as an unavoidable sequel to the death of God, informing us in the conclusion to *The Order of Things* that "Man" is an invention of recent date, soon to be erased, like a face drawn in sand at the edge of the sea. The demise announced by Nietzsche and Foucault, both that of God and Man, is of course no ordinary dying. It is rather the death of a conceptual construct, a dismantling of the scaffolding of elusive categories that portrays divinity as a supernatural being and defines the human self as a strange empirico-transcendental doublet, nestled in the hollow of self-effacing oppositions. It is thus that from the very beginning of what we have come to call postmodernism, the philosophical and the theological were destined to become entwined.

In my most recent work, *The Self after Postmodernity,* I developed a response to the postmodern announcement of the death of Man, as interpreted by Foucault, and the "deconstruction of the subject," as proposed by Heidegger and Derrida. Although being of one mind with the proponents of postmodernity in their problematizing of the classical metaphysical concept of the self as a firmly entrenched substance and the modern epistemological version of the subject as an Archimedean epistemic foundation, I nonetheless argued for a more robust self-understanding and self-constitution than postmodernists would allow. It was my considered assessment in this previous work that the death of Man/subject/self had been unduly exaggerated. I argued that in the wake of the deconstruction of the foundationalist prejudices of classical and modern metaphysics and epistemology a new self arises, like the Phoenix from its ashes, in the form and dynamics of a "who" of discourse, action, community, and transcendence. The death of the subject as abstract *hypokeimenon* and epistemological zero-point origin does not herald a foreclosure of all discourse about the self. It is rather a harbinger of a renewed and reconfigured self that answers to the questions *Who* is speaking? *Who* is acting? *Who* exists in community with others? and *Who* is exposed to transcendence?

In the current work, the corresponding thematic of postmodernity, that of the death of God, provides if not the principal focus at least a convenient, albeit arbitrary, starting point. As in my analysis and assessment of the death of the subject, so also in the present inquiry I examine the announcement of the death of the Deity to see if perchance, like the proclamation of the death of the human subject, it may not have been somewhat premature. But before making a judgment about the consequences of the announcement, it is necessary to arrive at some understanding of what it is that is announced. The ensuing format follows a trajectory similar to that of my previous project of resuscitating the life of the deconstructed self. After a critical assessment of the traditional metaphysical categories and epistemological criteria that have been placed in the service of theological construction, an effort is made to refigure the traditional concept of the Deity and to retrieve a viable content for religion as a form of communicative praxis.

It surely would be presumptuous on my part to be as bold as Kant is in the preface to the second edition of his *Critique of Pure Reason*, where he informs the reader that he has undertaken the dismantling of metaphysical knowledge about God, freedom, and immortality "in order to make room for *faith.*" Somewhat less assured of the consequences of my efforts in the following pages, I have a more modest intention to highlight some possibilities for a discourse that might enable one to talk about God in a renewed manner after two millennia of critical inquiry on matters of divinity. God-talk, I will attempt to show, resists reduction to abstract assertive claims about being and nonbeing, existence and nonexistence, substance and attributes. God-talk takes on the lineaments of a narrative, a story contextualized within the speech and action that make up the holistic history of our communicative praxis. My project thus takes shape as a search for a new grammar that might enable us to talk and write about matters of divinity in the present age.

This new grammar and discourse, as promised in the title of the present work, revolves around talk of God as "otherwise than being" and a proposal for a "semantics of the gift." Admittedly, these expressions have already made their way into the vocabulary of some current philosophical and theological reflection, and they may indeed have a history in a tradition that has been largely forgotten. In recent times Emmanuel Levinas in particular gave currency to talk about otherwise than being; however, as a careful scholar of the history of philosophy he was clearly cognizant of the role the expression already played in Plato's *Republic*. The grammar of "gift" has become virtually a household topic in certain contemporary philosophical and theological circles. Much of this may indeed be the result of Derrida bringing the phenomenon to the forefront in some of his recent writings.

Even a philosophical novitiate, however, knows that the concept of the gift is not a recent invention in the discipline. Interest in the phenomena of giving and receiving gifts extends all the way back to some of the earliest literature in Western thought, particularly to that in the Judeo-Christian tradition. Hence, the "new" discourse I am proposing for the examination of the topic of the current thought experiment is new only in a relative sense. Like all philosophical discourses, it proceeds against the backdrop of the ongoing conversation of humankind. But in revisiting the notion of the gift in an effort to articulate its bearing upon the God-question, I problematize some of the taken-for-granted concepts of gift giving and experiment with some new trajectories of interpretation. In particular, I delimit the usefulness of the vocabularies of reciprocity and reward in speaking of giving and receiving. I am also motivated to explore some possible refigurations of the ethical as it relates to the religious. And I experiment with new ways to talk about time as it relates to the gift. My hope is that in these efforts I have succeeded in saying something about the designated topic that has not yet been said. It is, of course, up to the reader to judge whether such has been accomplished.

There are five individuals who have read earlier drafts of the manuscript and have offered numerous helpful critical suggestions and need specifically to be acknowledged in my prefatory remarks: Michael J. Hyde, David James Miller, Stephen Thomas Pluháček, Ramsey Eric Ramsey, and

Sarah Elizabeth Roberts. Currently colleagues in the profession, they are all former students, once again providing support for the adage that one learns more from one's students and colleagues than one either realizes or is willing to admit. I would be remiss in failing to acknowledge Professor Eugene Long of the University of South Carolina and Professor William L. Rowe of Purdue University for their roles in both the genesis and the shaping of the present volume. As president of the Metaphysical Society of America, Professor Long invited me to present a paper at the annual meeting of the society in the spring of 1998, which had as its general theme "Religious Experience and Philosophical Reflection." My presentation at that meeting, "The Problem of Being and the Question about God," marked the beginning of the present study. Professor Rowe, a specialist in philosophy of religion, has been my colleague at Purdue since the early sixties. Living the paradox of being an ordained minister and a proponent of "friendly atheism," he has taught me much about the vagaries of classical theism. Pamela J. Connelly and Elaine Klemme of the Purdue University clerical staff are due special recognition for facilitating the smooth progression of the manuscript through cyberspace. I am grateful for the assistance by my daughter, Heather Schrag Stampfl, in the tiresome task of proofreading the typeset manuscript.

GOD AS OTHERWISE THAN BEING

PART   1

GOD AND BEING

1

The Problem of Being
and the Question about God

Metaphysics and Theism

The linkage of the problem of being and the question about God has been one of the more durable features of the legacies of philosophical and theological reflection in the history of Western thought. From the time of Aristotle's definition of God as "unmoved mover" in book lambda of his *Metaphysics* to Nietzsche's resounding proclamation of the "death of God" in *Thus Spake Zarathustra,* philosophy has been able to secure a placc in its agenda for inquiries into the existence and nature of God. These inquiries developed against the backdrop of certain metaphysical schema and categories that were quickly appropriated by theology for the purpose of articulating the defining attributes of a supernatural being. It is thus that reflection on the meaning and reality of what in the history of religion has been variously named the "divine," the "sacred," and the "holy" found a convenient semantic matrix in the grammar of a metaphysics of theism.

It may not be that simple to pin down with much degree of specificity the meaning of *theism,* given its multiple expressions. However, somewhat at the center of the theistic project are beliefs and associated practices pertaining to the existence and nature of a supreme being (or beings). Insofar as theism, particularly in Western philosophy and religion, has taken principally a monotheistic turn, theists have pursued the question about God from the perspective of a metaphysics of theism designed to inquire about the existence and status of *a* being. Plainly enough, the being that here becomes the object of investigation is not an ordinary sort of being one stumbles upon in doing an inventory of the furniture of the world encountered in mundane preoccupations. It is a distinctive kind of being. Using the resources of a metaphysical grammar, it is a being defined as infinite rather than finite, eternal rather than temporal, immutable rather than changeable, fully actual rather than in any respect potential, incorporeal without trace of matter, and devoid of anything imperfect in its absolute perfection.

These are the principal metaphysical attributes that have been ascribed to God, receiving a categorial consolidation in the medieval concept of the *ens realissimum*. This set the stage for Saint Anselm's well-known and oft-quoted characterization of God as that being than which nothing greater can be conceived. The rostrum of divine attributes that became normative for medieval theology also informed Saint Thomas Aquinas's five-fold definition of God as prime mover, first efficient cause, necessary being, supreme instance of perfection, and telic, or final, cause. This conceptual scaffolding and coupling of divine attributes continued into the modern era and was given expression in Descartes' one-liner on the nature of God as a supremely perfect being and Spinoza's designation of God as infinite substance. All of these definitions and characterizations of God, from the time of the ancients through the time of the moderns, move about within the vocabulary of a metaphysics of theism, informed by a rather bold application of the categories of essence and existence, substance and attribute, act and potency, form and matter, causality and dependence.

Since the advent of modernity, particularly since the time of Hegel, it has become a requirement of departments of philosophy and schools of theology to deal with the above issues in a special discipline flagged as "philosophy of religion." Courses taught under this rubric are for the most part formatted along the lines of metaphysics of theism. Sometimes authors of philosophy of religion texts group the selections from a list of principal contributors that includes Augustine, Anselm, Aquinas, Descartes, Spinoza, Leibniz, Hume, Kant, and Hegel under the designation "classical theism." The lead questions in the standard courses in this special discipline have to do with the existence and nature of a divine being and the relation of this being to the world. What are the essential features of such a divine being? What are the philosophical grounds for asserting that such a being exists? How is such a being, allegedly infinite, related to a finite world? If this divine being is understood to be absolutely good in its ultimate normativity, how can we account for the existence of evil among the finite beings the divine being in some sense produced, caused, or created?

These are some of the demanding questions that propel the basic inquiries in philosophy of religion. And we quickly note that these inquiries require the resources of metaphysics for their intelligibility. One asserts—or denies—the "existence" of such an entity. One devises a table of "attributes" to define the entity's "essence." One applies the category of "causality" to explain the relation of the divine entity to the empirical world. One solicits categories of "ideality" to get a grip on the perplexing problem of evil. The vocabularies of existence, attributes, essence, causality, and ideality all bespeak a close alliance with the metaphysical enterprise. We thus see how theology as the logos, the word, the discourse about God becomes linked to an inquiry into the meaning, structure, and modes of being.

It is necessary to proceed with some caution in an investigation of this linkage, which purports to unify in some manner the constructs of metaphysics and the interests of religion. The terrains of each of these disciplines are not that evenly terraced. Even in the relatively standardized format of philosophy of religion, there are varied approaches and perspectives. To be sure, the metaphysics of theism marks out much of the topography of the discipline. Yet, there are also putatively nonmetaphysical approaches to religious beliefs and practices. We have learned from the likes of Tertullian, Pascal, Kierkegaard, and Karl Barth that there is a distinction of some consequence between the God of the philosophers and the God of Abraham, Isaac, and Jacob. God defined as first cause and infinite substance may not that easily translate into God as revealed in decisive historical events. And there may indeed be some question as to whether this distinction, and others of this sort, beckon us beyond the parameters of a philosophical inquiry per se.

There is also the tradition of mysticism, which has made an impact on both Western and Eastern religious thought and in which the linkage of metaphysics and theology becomes somewhat more tenuous. The life of the mystic testifies of an immediate and ineffable encounter with a Deity that defies any categorial determinations. Ordinary epistemic signifiers and communicable descriptions appear to be left behind. Yet, the linkage with epistemology and metaphysics is never entirely severed. Indeed, a careful examination of the highly personalized vocabulary of classical mysticism will show that the mystical for the most part continues to reside in the metaphysical, evidenced in the mystics' employment of locutions that continue to make purchases on the binary metaphysical grammar of infinity versus finitude, eternality versus temporality, and nonmateriality versus materiality.

As the terrain of philosophy of religion is unevenly contoured, so is the landscape of metaphysics, on which classical theism has staked out a rather encompassing region for its claims. From even a hurried survey of the history of philosophy we learn that no solid consensus on the task and scope of metaphysics has been forthcoming. Differing and sometimes opposing answers have been given to the question, What is metaphysics?

Textbooks designed to introduce students to this formidable discipline often delineate different types of metaphysics, issuing from different philosophical persuasions or schools of thought. These include idealist metaphysics, realist metaphysics, naturalist metaphysics, romanticist metaphysics, existential metaphysics, garden varieties of each, and in some cases combinations of them all. Although helpful at times, the limitations of such a typological approach to the discipline has been well documented in the profession. Typological classification, reinforced by the multiplication of philosophical "isms," simply does not get us all that far.

There are good reasons to begin with Aristotle when dealing with matters metaphysical. He was responsible for the first philosophical treatise bearing the explicit title *Metaphysics.* And although the title was simply a bibliographical designation, indexing the work that "came after" the *Physics,* the contents under discussion in the work became normative for subsequent metaphysical inquiry. At issue in metaphysical inquiry is the problem of being. Admittedly this problem had already become a topic for philosophical reflection before the time of Aristotle. Plato's *Sophist* is frequently referenced as Plato's dialogue in which the meaning of being becomes an explicit theme, particularly as it is developed against the backdrop of an investigation of the interplay of being and nonbeing and the role of this interplay in moderating the opposition of sameness and otherness, identity and difference. The contribution of Plato to inquiries regarding the meaning of being has been recalled for us by Heidegger in the opening line of *Being and Time,* where he quotes from the *Sophist:* "For manifestly you have long been aware of what you mean when you use the expression '*being*'. We however, who used to think we understand it, have now become perplexed."[1]

It was in the Aristotelian corpus, however, that the categorial machinery for the pursuit of the problem of being was set in place. Metaphysics as the inquiry into the problem of "being qua being" (*on ē on*), as Aristotle defines the discipline in book gamma, proceeds via an investigation making use of the categorial schemes of substance and attribute, actuality and potentiality, form and matter, causality and dependence. An application of these categorial schemes is to yield nothing less than a complete inventory of any being in question.

But at the very heart of the proposed metaphysical inquiry into the problem of being, there resides a curious ambiguity. The problem of "being qua being" can be formulated on the one hand as an inquiry into

1. Martin Heidegger, *Being and Time,* trans. John Macquarrie and Edward Robinson (New York: Harper and Row, 1962), 1.

the different kinds and modes of being comprising a totality of causal interconnectedness. On the other hand, the inquiry can move in the direction of an investigation of the meaning of *to be* as it is illustrated in each of the beings that make up the inventory of what there is.

It is well known that in book lambda of the *Metaphysics* the narrative provides an account of the highest kind of being (*timiōtaton genos*), which finds its quintessential exemplification in the pure actuality of God as unmoved mover. Aristotle's *Metaphysics* thus finds its climax in the emplotment of a theology that tells the story of the unmoved mover as the completion of the project as set forth in book gamma. In this journey from an interrogation of "being qua being" to the discovery of the highest kind of being, we traverse a landscape in which different kinds, or modes, of being have been sorted out and their relations to each other explained.

That the trajectory in the exploration of the being-problem points in the direction of the highest being, God as unmoved mover, providing a causal explanation in the guise of an ultimate telic principle that explains the movement in all of the lower forms of being, should come as no surprise. If the guiding question is, What are the peculiar attributes of the different substances and why do these substances exist at all in the manner in which they do exist? then a theo-metaphysical format will be set in place. The impact this theo-metaphysical stance had upon medieval philosophy, indeed upon all subsequent forms of theism, can hardly be overemphasized.

The other facet of the being-problem as posed by Plato and Aristotle, however, should not be overlooked. Instead of the inquiry moving in the direction of a comprehension of the totality of beings, each being with its defining attributes and each somehow causally connected with other beings, the inquiry instead interrogates the way or manner in which each of these beings, in referential togetherness, are. Here the being-problem takes on a different point of departure and a different goal, proceeding from the inquiry standpoint of what it means "to be." Particular beings, whether human, animal, vegetable, or mineral, "exist" in a certain way as they stand out from nonbeing. It is the "to be" of the human self, the gazelle, the rose, and the rock that marks each entity off from nonbeing. These complementing inquiries, one inquiring into the totality of beings as causally connected and the other inquiring into the meaning of "to be," have been at work throughout the tradition, although they have not always been that clearly sorted out.

Since the time of Heidegger in particular, it is common to refer to these two inquiries as the ontic and the ontological, respectively. Ontic inquiry addresses matters having to do with particular beings or entities (*Seiendes*) in their totality and causal interdependence. Ontological inquiry investigates the Being (*Sein*) of these beings. It probes the "to be" of their entitative status, the manner or way in which they show themselves or come to presence. It is the view of Heidegger that Western metaphysics has mainly followed the route of ontic inquiry, and consequently it has preoccupied itself with an investigation of the different kinds of being and the peculiar relations that obtain among them, comprising some manner of unity and totality.[2] It is thus that metaphysics became oriented toward a comprehension of what Arthur Lovejoy perceptively named "the great chain of being." The different orders, levels, or gradations of being illustrate a binding texture along a scale of subordination of the lower to the higher.

It is not all that surprising that medieval theology would find a comfortable residence within the edifice of the great chain of being, given its proclivity toward a synthesis of Christian theology and Greek philosophy. The highest being, to which all lower forms of being are subordinated, became a suitable candidate for the main designators that medieval theologians assigned to God. Within the nexus of links that comprise the great chain of being, God was positioned at the summit of a vast celestial hierarchy. Saint Thomas Aquinas's celebrated "five ways" illustrates this quite dramatically. The highest being is first mover, prime efficient cause, necessary existent, supreme instance of perfection, and cosmic designer—and all of these, concludes Aquinas, is what we appropriately call God. After having demonstrated the existence of such a highest being, we can then invoke the classical substance-attribute schema to delineate the metaphysical attributes that make up the portrait of divinity. These include eternality, pure actuality, incorporeality, immutability, absolute simplicity, impassibility, omniscience, omnipotence, and omnibenevolence. The next project is to graft on to these metaphysical attributes the distinctive religious attributes (such as creator, lord, judge, and redeemer), thus advancing the concordance of Athens and Jerusalem.

This merger of metaphysical and religious attributes against the backdrop of the developing synthesis of Greek philosophy and Judeo-Christian theology spawned a peculiar epistemological problem that was destined to travel with the metaphysics of theism far into the modern period. This was the problem of the relation of faith and reason. Knowledge of the metaphysical attributes is apparently accessible to the human mind by virtue of the natural light of reason. But the specifically religious

2. See particularly Martin Heidegger's essay "The Way Back into the Ground of Metaphysics," in *Existentialism from Dostoevsky to Sartre,* ed. Walter Kaufmann (New York: Meridian Books, 1956), 206–21.

attributes, which have to do mainly with God's revelation and action in history, remain within the province of faith. It was thus the stage was set for the seemingly interminable squabbles regarding the alignment—or in some cases, nonalignment—of faith and reason. What relation obtains between the two? Are they complementary? Do they stand in a relation of mutual reinforcement? Does faith somehow complete reason, analogous to the then commonly accepted view that grace completes nature? Or do the two stand in a relation of unbridgeable opposition? It is here in particular we are able to discern the emergence of the epistemological problematic that became such a bugbear in the modern period of classical theism.

An often overlooked footnote in the story of medieval theo-metaphysics, which itself had a significant impact on the formulation of the epistemological problematic, involves the writings of a fifth-century Neoplatonist, Pseudo-Dionysius Areopagita, usually considered to be one of the more articulate spokespersons for "negative theology." His work *On Divine Names* was particularly influential. The lynchpin in his negative theology had to do with the indescribability of the nature of God. To indicate this indescribability, we have to employ certain self-negating locutions. We can indeed speak of God as "Superessential Essence" and "Superexisting Deity," but in doing so we need to be constantly reminded that our efforts to say what God is culminate in a *via negativa* of saying what he is not. God is not "Essence" and he is not "Existence"—at least not in any of the philosophical senses that one might recognize. Yet, this must not be construed as the utterance of a simple negation. The not-being of this and that is not the assertion of an absence. It is rather a serendipitous effort to point to the superabundance or surplus of the divine majesty.

There are clearly in the negative theology of Pseudo-Dionysius shades of Plato's requirement in the *Republic* to think "beyond" or "otherwise than" being construed as essence, idea, or form. This was a requirement that was enthusiastically embraced by Neoplatonism, and assuredly Pseudo-Dionysius stands in this tradition. But he also embraced the Christian faith. And like Saint Augustine before him, he sought a rapprochement of Neoplatonism with Christianity. However, whereas Augustine transmuted Neoplatonic teachings into Christian doctrines, Pseudo-Dionysius inverted the vectors of the relation in his attempt to find a place for Christianity within the vision of Neoplatonic philosophy.

The relevance of the account of Pseudo-Dionysius for our own narrative has to do principally with his insertion of negative theology into the mix of a metaphysics of theism and its impact on the problem of the knowledge of God. That this problem should have taken center stage in modernity, the legacy of which is the effecting of the epistemological turn, hardly comes as a surprise. Nor is it surprising that references to Pseudo-Dionysius and negative theology should recur in postmodernist literature. It is of some moment to point out that because of suggested similarities between the strategy of deconstruction and the *via negativa,* Derrida was forced to address the issue head-on, mounting a disclaimer to the view that the one translates into the other. "What I write is not 'negative theology'," insists Derrida, maintaining that deconstruction parts company with negative theology "in the measure to which 'negative theology' seems to reserve, beyond all positive predication, beyond all negation, even beyond Being, some hyperessentiality, a being beyond Being."[3] Deconstruction and negative theology both display an intensified sensitivity to ways of speaking about that which one purports to speak, and both recognize the role of negation and denial in human discourse. But the *via negativa* has a different function in the two approaches. Negative theology lays claim to a superabundance or excess of Being by attesting in a quite serendipitous manner to "a being beyond Being." If such is indeed the case, then it would need to be said that even the denials within negative theology are unable to escape the strictures of a metaphysical grammar. Whereas the denials within deconstruction "defer" all determinations of being in its positivity as presence, negative theology continues to reside in the hollow of a metaphysics of theism.

Although one is able to identify a pivotal feature of theism as having to do with the claim that there exists a supreme being, ultimately normative and self-sufficient, in some manner independent of the world of nature and history, it is necessary to keep in mind that there are both doctrinal variations and differing popular expressions within the wide framework of theism. Paul Tillich in sketching his project of "transcending theism" has been particularly helpful in sorting out some different meanings and uses of theism.

There is first what Tillich calls theism as "the unspecified affirmation of God." This is a form of nonreflective theism, a theism bound up with accepted and taken-for-granted usages and accumulated psychological connotations in talking about God. This is the theism to which politicians often appeal in their rhetorical designs to invoke a mood of reverence to assure the public that their views are in accord with the highest standards of morality. "Politicians, dictators, and other people who wish to use rhetoric to make an impression on their audience like to

3. Jacques Derrida, "How to Avoid Speaking: Denials," in *Derrida and Negative Theology,* ed. Harold Coward and Toby Foshay (Albany: State University of New York Press, 1992), 77.

use the word God in this sense," says Tillich. "It produces the feeling in their listeners that the speaker is serious and morally trustworthy. This is especially successful if they can brand their foes as atheistic."[4] This meaning of theism, avers Tillich, is basically empty in content and for the most part remains benign and innocuous.

The second meaning of theism is more substantive, having to do with what Tillich calls "the divine-human encounter," expressive of certain elements in the Judeo-Christian tradition that accentuate the person-to-person relationship in speaking of God, emphasizing the personalistic image of the Deity and coming down heavy on the nature of human faith and divine forgiveness. This second type of theism displays a concreteness in its use of psychologically based descriptions that borders on a personalistic literalism, and because of this it stands in danger of inviting an anthropomorphism that would divest the concept of God of all religious content.

The third type of theism is the most onerous of the three. The meaning of this third type is a strictly theological and philosophical one, dependent upon a conceptualization designed to prove the existence of God in some manner and define his constitutive features. It is the view of Tillich that all three types of theism need to be transcended. The first should be transcended because it is irrelevant for a disciplined inquiry into the meaning of God, the second because it overextends the grammar of "divine-human encounter," and the third because it is philosophically and theologically unsound. "Theism in the third sense must be transcended because it is wrong," he says. "It is bad theology. This can be shown by a more penetrating analysis. The God of theological theism is a being beside others and as such a part of the whole of reality. He certainly is considered its most important part, but as a part and therefore as subjected to the structure of the whole. He is supposed to be beyond the ontological elements and categories which constitute reality. But every statement subjects him to them. He is seen as a self which has a world, as an ego which is related to a thou, as a cause which is separated from its effect, as having a definite space and an endless time."[5]

It is quite clear that what is at issue in Tillich's third type of theism is the portrait of the Deity as framed against the backdrop of what Heidegger has felicitously called "the onto-theo-logical constitution of metaphysics."[6] When theology and metaphysics become entwined, God

---

4. Paul Tillich, *The Courage to Be* (New Haven, Conn.: Yale University Press, 1952), 182.

5. Ibid., 184.

6. Martin Heidegger, *Identity and Difference*, trans. Joan Stambaugh (New York: Harper and Row, 1969), 42–74.

is depicted as a being among other beings, an entity among other entities, filling out the space that comprises the totality of all entities. To be
sure, as Tillich notes, God is considered to be the most important part
of the totality, but a part nonetheless, subordinated to the structure of
the whole. It is also of some significance to be reminded that Tillich's
reflections on the meaning of God follow certain lines marked out by
Heidegger's elaboration of the ontic/ontological difference. The Tillich-
Heidegger connection would be a possible and important topic for a
specific research project, but it is one we will not be able to pursue in
the present essay. Suffice it to observe that Heidegger did play a role in
shaping Tillich's systematic theology. Any ontic analysis, which according to Heidegger becomes the task of metaphysics and which proceeds
as an interrogation of the categorial structure of beings that make up
the furniture of the universe, is destined to come up lame in addressing
the question about God.

It is thus that for Tillich the concept of God in the history of the
metaphysics of theism, which has been destined to follow the trajectories
of ontic analysis and construction, falls out not only as philosophically
untenable but also religiously pernicious. It is this concept, according
to Tillich, that Nietzsche confronted in his declaration of the death of
God. Supplying the lynchpin for a theo-metaphysical portrait of God,
this concept of *theo* particularly needs to be transcended, because it leads
to the reduction of the Deity to an invincible tyrant who controls all of
the lower orders of being through an exercise of absolute knowledge
and power and in doing so invites a justifiable atheism. "This is the God
that Nietzsche said had to be killed because nobody can tolerate being
made into mere objects of absolute knowledge and absolute control,"
Tillich states. "This is the deepest root of atheism. It is an atheism that
is justified as the reaction against theological theism and its disturbing
implications."[7]

After the failure of metaphysics to secure a philosophically and
theologically viable concept of the Deity, the question of course arises
whether fundamental ontology with its ontological analysis might do the
job where ontic analysis came up short. There are times and places Tillich
suggests such might be the case. In *Systematic Theology*, Tillich does not
hesitate to use the vocabulary of "God as Being." To be sure, he remains
consistent in his view that God should not be understood as an existent
being alongside other existent beings, even if accorded the highest exemplification of existence; but apparently the grammar of being can still

7. Tillich, *The Courage to Be*, 185.

be utilized in our discourse about God. "The being of God is being-itself," Tillich writes. "The being of God cannot be understood as the existence of a being alongside others or above others. If God is *a* being, he is subject to the categories of finitude, especially to space and substance."[8] Ontic descriptions no longer apply, but apparently ontological ones still do. God is being-itself. Furthermore, we are enjoined to read the statement, "God is being-itself," as literal rather than symbolic. "The statement that God is being-itself is a nonsymbolic statement," he continues. "It does not point beyond itself. It means what it says directly and properly; if we speak of the actuality of God, we first assert that he is not God if he is not being-itself. . . . Theologians must make explicit what is implicit in religious thought and expression; and, in order to do this, they must begin with the most abstract and completely unsymbolic statement which is possible, namely that God is being-itself or the absolute."[9]

Tillich's philosophical theology, some of the sources of which can be found in classical German Idealism, continues to rely on the resources of a vocabulary of being. God is being-itself. The epistemology that grounds this philosophical theology pivots on an explicit doctrine of the religious symbol. Religious knowledge is symbolic through and through. However, in response to a number of critics on this issue, Tillich was persuaded to modify his position so as to allow for nonsymbolic knowledge of God. "An early criticism by Professor Urban of Yale," Tillich tells us, "forced me to acknowledge that in order to speak of symbolic knowledge one must delimit the symbolic realm by an unsymbolic statement. I was grateful for this criticism, and under its impact I became suspicious of any attempts to make the concept of the symbol all-embracing and therefore meaningless. The unsymbolic statement which implies the necessity of religious symbolism is that God is being-itself, and as such beyond the subject-object structure of everything that is."[10]

Tillich's doctrine of the symbol as it relates to religious knowledge and theological grammar is particularly instructive for highlighting one of the more knotty epistemological problems that travel with a metaphysics of theism even when one makes an effort, as does Tillich, to think beyond it. The move on the part of Tillich to anchor symbolic language about God in a nonsymbolic statement is reminiscent of the aporia in the medieval doctrine of analogy, in which it became evident that to deliver

8. Paul Tillich, *Systematic Theology*, vol. 1 (Chicago: University of Chicago Press, 1951), 235.

9. Ibid., 239.

10. Charles W. Kegley and Robert W. Bretall, eds., *The Theology of Paul Tillich* (New York: Macmillan, 1952), 334.

informative analogical predications about God one would have to appeal to a univocal predication somewhere down the line.

A similar state of affairs surfaces in a consideration of the connection of the metaphorical with the literal, the figurative with the proper. These are matters that continue to perplex not only the advocates of classical theism, but also epistemologists and philosophers of language more generally. How does the symbolic, the analogical, the metaphorical, the figurative fraternize with the nonsymbolic, the univocal, the literal, and the proper? Might one after considerable analysis and interpretation be able to say of the symbolic and the analogical what Heidegger has said about the metaphorical, namely that it continues to reside in the metaphysical?[11]

The aggressive embrace of ontological grammar and a reliance on the distinction between the symbolic and the nonsymbolic in discourse about God on the part of Tillich would appear to make the Heidegger-Tillich connection considerably more tenuous, particularly so if we recall Heidegger's statements that faith has no need for the thinking of Being and that if he ever were to write a book on theology the word *Being* would not appear. Yet, the matter is not all that easily decidable, for in his "Letter on Humanism" Heidegger informs the reader that it is only against the backdrop of the truth of Being that the essence of the holy and the essence of divinity can be thought and that we can learn what the word *God* signifies.[12] It would thus seem that even for Heidegger there is a connection of some significance between the truth of Being and the question about God. What this connection is remains to be sorted out, and doing so will require that we attend to the fate of the ontic/ontological difference against the backdrop of the linguistic turn in the philosophy of Heidegger and in the story of twentieth-century philosophy more generally.

The Epistemological and Linguistic Turns

One of the characteristic marks of the period known as modern philosophy was the privileging of the problem of knowledge. Descartes is commonly credited with having defined the inquiry standpoint that marked

11. Heidegger, "Das Metaphorische gibt es nur innerhalbe der Metaphysik," *Der Satz vom Grund* (Günther Neske Pfullingen, 1958), 89.
12. Martin Heidegger, "Letter on Humanism," *Martin Heidegger: Basic Writings.*, rev. ed., ed. David Farrell Krell (San Francisco: HarperSanFrancisco, 1993), 230.

the transition from the medieval to the modern period. He was of the conviction that to do philosophy in a way that can produce compelling results requires that one first systematically lay out the rules of procedure and the criteria of truth that are to govern the investigation. It is a requirement of modernity that the first task is to set one's epistemological house in order. Commonly we speak of this requirement as a signal for the epistemological turn. That a linguistic turn would follow on the heels of the epistemological turn somewhat later was surely to be expected.

The effects of the combined epistemological and linguistic turns in the development of modernity were prominently inscribed in each of the special disciplines that make up the philosophical enterprise. Thus, philosophy of religion, which was soon to become a specific field of inquiry, was unable to avoid the demand for epistemological responsibility in dealing with its subject matter. Having inherited a concept of God from traditional metaphysics of theism, the task then became that of providing epistemological warrant for knowledge of such a supreme being. That this was a formidable task goes without saying. It became increasingly difficult for knowledge about God to meet the test of the modern, more specifically the Enlightenment, criteria for knowing.

To meet this challenge, various arguments for the existence of God were marshaled. These included the cosmological, the ontological, the teleological, and the moral arguments. Much of the format in standard courses in the philosophy of religion is devoted to a careful examination and evaluation of these arguments. To be sure, these arguments in one form or another had already found a place in ancient and medieval thought, but they now had to be tailored to follow the prescriptions of modern epistemological theory. These prescriptions revolved around a criteriological conception of rationality that linked criteria to strict methodological requirements and set its sights on unimpeachable standards for epistemic justification.

Criteria and method were seen as two sides of the same coin. This was already prefigured in Descartes's promulgation of the "rules of method" that are to govern philosophical inquiry, in which the rule of certainty supplied the criteria of clarity and distinctness as the reliable guides for epistemic justification. Only by sticking with the rules of method, which prescribe in advance the criteria for certainty, will we be able to achieve a secure foundation for knowledge in the special sciences. It is thus that at the very beginning of the modern period the machinery for an epistemological foundationalism was set in operation. To achieve an accurate representation of what there is in the world, we need to front-load reliable criteria against which our various representations can then be measured. Whether the rules of method dictate that these criteria are clear and distinct ideas (as in Cartesian rationalism) or whether they land upon discrete sense impressions (as in British empiricism)—profound though the differences in the end might be—does not as such violate the project of a foundationalism that elevates method and criteria for epistemic justification to the status of a first principle.

Kant's position with regard to the epistemological problematic in modernity remains somewhat singular, given his effort to accommodate the requirements of both rationalism and empiricism. However, the itch for epistemological foundations remained intact. It was not that rationalists and empiricists erred in looking for foundations; they erred in not looking for them in the right place. What is required to garner the foundations of knowledge, according to Kant, is a determination of its transcendental roots—and more precisely its roots in a "transcendental unity of apperception" which directs the syntheses of apprehension in perception, schematization via the workings of the imagination, and recognition in conception. The recognition in conception is made possible by virtue of the twelve categories that govern the rules of inquiry and the availability of a table of judgments that prescribes in advance the criteria for evaluating knowledge claims. These knowledge claims need to pass the test of either analytical–a priori, synthetical–a priori, or synthetical–a posteriori validation. Categories resident a priori in the mind and a strategy of conceptualization based on a quite specific theory of judgment provide the methodological protocols for a transcendental theory of knowledge.

It was to be expected that this privileging of method, rule-governed procedures, and predelineated criteria by proponents of rationalism and empiricism alike would incline philosophers to look to the natural sciences for the touchstone of what it means to be rational. This led to a rather profound narrowing of the range and scope of reason. *Rational, scientific, objective,* and *verifiable* came to be considered virtually synonymous. To be rational, given such fraternization with scientific objectivity, is to set one's sights on knowledge that is subject to controlled verificationist procedures—either to the strict verificationist criteria of positivism or to somewhat more charitable feedback and control mechanisms. In any event, the epistemological protocols of modernity courted a notion of "technical" reason that did not fit all that well with the more encompassing "ontological" reason of the ancients and the medievals that was based on a metaphysically anchored logos doctrine. The disposition of the modern mind was to emancipate logic from the logos and to restrict the reach of knowledge to objectifiable data.

The declaration of autonomy by modern logic, liberating it from the claims and promises within the ancient and medieval doctrine of the logos, may well constitute the main motivational factor in the epistemological turn of modernity. The effect of this sundering of logic and logos had considerable consequence for the newly founded discipline of philosophy of religion, particularly as it impacted on the classical arguments for the existence of God. The uses of logic exemplified, for example, in Anselm's celebrated ontological "proof" continued to be informed by the resources of a logos that was able to apprehend the structure of reality and maintain a correlativity of being and the good. The ancient logos doctrine, which Hans-Georg Gadamer has aptly characterized as "the grand hypothesis of Greek philosophy," taught that there was an unbroken solidarity between the cosmos and the human soul. Rationality was understood principally as a unifying power within the structure of being itself, and only secondarily as an abstractable property of the human mind.[13]

Given this close connection between the mind and the cosmos, rationality as the exercise of the logos is accorded an explicit ontological determination. The human mind is "logical" insofar as it participates in the "logos" as the rational structure of the cosmos. Conjoined with this ontological perspective on rationality was the Platonic and Augustinian coupling of being and good. "*Esse qua esse bonum est*" is Saint Augustine's well-known one-liner on the issue. Plainly enough, without these two ontological commitments issuing from the Greek exaltation of the logos doctrine, Anselm's so-called proof for the existence of a being than which nothing greater can be conceived would hardly have gotten off the ground.

The consequences of the separation of logic from logos and the ensuing preoccupation with technical and controlling knowledge for a devaluation of the fortunes of metaphysics are very much a part of the dynamics of the modern mind. Hume's empirically based skepticism and Kant's sustained critique of classical metaphysics are two of the most prominent expressions of a revolt against the enterprise of metaphysics as defined by the ancients and the medievals. To be sure, Hume's empiricistic skepticism was more confrontational in dealing with traditional metaphysics than was Kant's transcendental philosophy. Hume was ready to commit to the flames any work in metaphysics or theology that could

---

13. "The rationality of being, this grand hypothesis of Greek philosophy, is not first and foremost a property of human self-consciousness but of being itself, which is the whole in such a way and appears as the whole in such a way that human reason is far more appropriately thought of as part of this rationality instead of as the self-consciousness that knows itself over against an external totality," Hans-Georg Gadamer, *Reason in the Age of Science*, trans. Frederick G. Lawrence (Cambridge, Mass.: MIT Press, 1984), 18.

not base its claims on knowledge of relations of ideas or matters of fact.[14] Kant was somewhat more charitable, agreeing with Hume that the days of dogmatic metaphysics were indeed over but also registering some concerns about a skepticism that tried to get along only with percepts. Admittedly, concepts without percepts are empty (the failure of traditional metaphysics), but equally, percepts without concepts are blind (the limitation of an empirically based skepticism). Nonetheless, in spite of some important disagreements between Hume and Kant on the possibilities and limitations of empirical knowledge, they were basically in accord that reason, given its diminished resources and narrowed focus, simply remained too poverty stricken to furnish knowledge about the structure, dynamics, and modes of being.

One of the more decisive implications of Kant's aggressive critique of pure reason for the concept of God in modernity involves the meaning and applicability of the category of existence in the designs of his transcendental philosophy. A telling strategy within Kant's Copernican revolution was that of analyzing the classical metaphysical category of existence into a category of human finitude, deflating its serviceability for the traditional proofs for the existence of God. The "is" of existence is not a property that attaches to an entity. Existence is not a predicate. Existence has rather to do with the determination of the status that an entity has within the manifold of time and space—a determination whereby the entity is marked off not simply from other entities (the determination of essence) but is marked off from nonexistence. In no way, runs Kant's argument, does the determination of existence enlarge one's conception of the entity or the subject in question. Hence, one must never confuse contingent judgments about existence with necessary judgments involving predication. To assert, for example, that "God is omnipotent" is to submit a necessary judgment, in which the predicate is directly entailed from the meaning of the subject. To assert, however, that "God exists" is to offer a contingent judgment, in which "exists" functions not as a predicate but rather as the determination that there is such an entity, "God," that has some species of status in reality. But it is precisely this status that is rendered problematic in the efforts of finite reason to achieve constitutive knowledge about putative realities in the noumenal realm.

14. "If we take in our hand any volume; of divinity or school metaphysics, for instance; let us ask, *Does it contain any abstract reasoning concerning quantity or number?* No. *Does it contain any experimental reasoning concerning matter of fact and existence?* No. Commit it then to the flames: for it can contain nothing but sophistry and illusion," David Hume, *Enquiries Concerning the Human Understanding and Concerning the Principles of Morals*, ed. L. A. Selby-Bigge (Oxford, England: Clarendon Press, 1902), 165.

The final consequences of Kant's refiguration of existence as a category of human finitude, determining the status of an entity within a spatio-temporal matrix, may well have not been followed through by Kant himself, given that he continued to speak of the "existence" of God as a regulative idea, one that could profitably be used in directing future inquiry on the subject. Clearly, according to Kant, we cannot lay claim to constitutive knowledge of the existence of God, a noumenal soul, or a unified cosmos. Finite reason abruptly encounters its limitations in seeking a unification of the subjective conditions of experience in a metaphysical doctrine of the soul, in seeking a unification of the objective conditions of experience in the idea of the cosmos, and in seeking a unification of both the subjective and objective conditions in the idea of God. The pursuit of the former lands us in a paralogism, the second in insurmountable antinomies, and the third in a transcendental illusion.

Yet, the three Ideas of Reason (the soul, cosmos, and God) remain for Kant conceptually viable even though they can never become objects of constitutive knowledge. This would appear to allow the acceptance of the traditional metaphysical concept of God as *a being,* as an entity with some superlative status about which existence-talk is still appropriate—even though, of course, any demonstrations of the existence of such an entity would remain forever outside the range and reach of pure reason. Admittedly, such talk about the existence of God cannot be literal. God's existence cannot be of the same stripe as the existence of finite entities within the spatio-temporal manifold. Hence, when one talks about the existence of God, one will need to speak analogically, metaphorically, symbolically—or possibly *via negativa.* If, however, Kant's refiguration of existence as a category of human finitude is taken somewhat more earnestly and more consistently, then one might be inclined to restrict its applicability to beings that come to presence in the sensory manifold and experiment with a discourse about God that furrows a path to that which is otherwise than beings, if not indeed otherwise than Being itself, transcending both the ontic and ontological designations of reality.

A far-reaching consequence of this narrowing of the scope of reason and indictment of metaphysical knowledge for the theological and religious disciplines was the intensification of the debates on reason versus faith. This was, of course, not a new issue or problem. It had already received a hearing in the Middle Ages. But now the conflict between these two "ways of knowing" appeared to reach a point of no return, the problem itself gravitating into a curious aporia. Although critical of the claims of metaphysics, modern philosophy of religion from Kant onward kept intact the concept of God as it was employed in theistic metaphysics. It was somehow accepted that such was indeed the proper way to define and characterize God—namely as a being, admittedly the highest being or that being than which nothing greater can be conceived, whose principal attributes consist of the old familiar ones of eternality, immutability, incorporeality, supreme perfection, and the like. Apparently no adjustments needed to be made with respect to the metaphysical status of God defined as an entity that in some sense "exists" and possesses a quite distinctive "essence."

However, "knowing" that such a being exists and has such a nature could not meet the test required by the Enlightenment criteria for knowledge. Hence, an adjustment needed to be made on the epistemological side of the ledger. Either we broaden the scope of knowledge achieved though technical reason (possibly by retrieving some of the resources of ontological reason as practiced by the ancients and medievals), or we simply abandon the uses of reason in achieving knowledge of God and place all of our bets on the resources of faith. The latter path is the one taken by fideism, namely that nothing about God, neither his existence nor his essence, can be known by the natural light of reason. Knowledge of God is *toute court* a matter of faith.

Yet, even this abandonment of the resources of reason and the reliance on faith continued to make purchases on the epistemological venture. Faith continued to function as a kind of latter-day epistemic mode of apprehension, tailored to fill the epistemological gap that was created as a result of the inability of technical reason to lay hold of truths about divine reality. Somewhat curiously, the "apprehension" of the intended object, namely the God of classical theism, became profoundly problematized, but the defining features of the putative object itself evaded scrutiny. The appeal to faith simply called for another route to knowledge of a highest being and thus remained quite firmly entrenched in the subject-object polarization of the modern epistemological paradigm. What was not asked about was whether the metaphysical scaffolding inherited from the ancients and the epistemological framework as invented by the moderns alike might not need to be questioned with respect to their usefulness when it comes to talking about God.

It was this suggestion to reexamine our God-talk that opened up a new perspective, a shift of inquiry if you will, from epistemological to linguistic concerns. Attention became focused specifically on the resources of language to which we appeal in our variegated ways of *speaking* about God, both on the part of the learned and the vulgar. The shift from the epistemological to the linguistic turn has of course been well documented in the literature. The later is a turn that was maneuvered on both sides of the English Channel. On the Continent it took the form of a turn to semiotics, more specifically structuralist linguistics. In Great Britain, thanks particularly to the later Wittgenstein, the linguistic turn came to be characterized as a turn to ordinary language. In both cases, the importance of language for philosophical analysis and exploration was given a new emphasis, although this new role for linguistic analysis continued a fragile liaison with the epistemological problematic of modernity.

This entwinement of linguistics and epistemology was readily discernible in the move to semiotics within the structuralist theory of knowledge. The signifier/signified dyad of structuralist linguistics takes on intelligibility only against the backdrop of the representational model of modern epistemology. Signifiers take the place of the role of mental acts intending contents of consciousness, and the signified stands in for the intended meaning and the indicated referent. However, given the polysemy in the play of signifying, indeed the convertibility of the signifier and the signified in the search for meaning and reference, all cards in the epistemological game appear to be stacked against any decidability of meaning and any satisfactory determination of reference. Hence, the epistemological requirement of locating that which the signifieds are to represent remains unfulfilled. Thus the move toward formalism in structural linguistics was not unexpected. The semiotic became disengaged from the semantic. Signifiers were absolved of the demand to deliver either meaning or reference. The functions of the sign were restricted to the specialized scientific subdisciplines of linguistics (phonemics, grammar, and syntax) that deal with an analysis of the elemental units of language, independent of their hermeneutical function in the disclosure of a speaker or author saying something to someone about something.

The consequences of the separation of the semiotic from the semantic for structuralism as a philosophy were quite far reaching. So long as structuralist analysis was confined to a science of linguistics, the abstraction of the semiotic from the semantic was warranted. There is no requirement that the specialized subdisciplines of linguistics as sciences need address issues having to do with the truth value of propositions and with speaker reference. Studies of phonemes, morphemes, and syntactical structure can happily proceed without asking questions about either the referents of sentential utterances or about the status of speakers. As sciences they quite legitimately abstract from such questions as, Who is speaking? and To what is the speaker referring when he or she speaks?

The terrain changes, however, when structuralism takes on the mantle of philosophy and attempts to deal with matters epistemological and ontological. In its effort to use semiotics to provide the infrastructural invariants on the basis of which the variations in the superstructure can be explained, structuralism as a philosophy lost both the subject and the hermeneutical referents of discourse. It was unable to come to terms either with questions of meaning and reference or the question concerning the speaking subject. It was thus Claude Lévi-Strauss's reply to Sartre on the goal of the human sciences became predictable. The ultimate goal of a science of man, says Lévi-Strauss, is "not to constitute, but to dissolve man."[15] With this proclamation, Lévi-Strauss voiced the structuralist position on the fate of the human subject. The subject has no place in a science of human behavior that has its sights set on an explanatory model of objective and invariant infrastructural relations within the sign-system of semiotics. If such is indeed the fate of the human subject, namely to be dissolved within the hollow of invariant signifiers and signifieds, then one will be able to expect little more when the fate of the Deity is at stake.

The ordinary language school in Great Britain, spearheaded principally by Ludwig Wittgenstein, Gilbert Ryle, and J. L. Austin, was more amenable to an analysis of religious language than was its Continental counterpart of structuralist linguistics. Although the proponents of ordinary language philosophy had been schooled in modern epistemology, particularly that of a positivist orientation, they quickly became dissatisfied with the narrowness of a criteriological conception of rationality that appealed to criteria that were laid out in advance and dissociated from linguistic performance. If the meanings of our varied expressions reside in the way we use language in our everyday, ordinary locutions and perlocutions, then it will behoove us to be done with criteria that are frontloaded. Criteria are *post festum;* they arise within the rough and tumble of our everyday efforts to communicate information about something to someone. The meaning of a word or a sentence in the deployment of our discourse resides in its use.

Criteria are thus divested of their affiliation with "theory of knowledge" and are relocated within a rhetorical space. They are seen to emerge from a speaker/hearer interaction. Appeals to incontrovertible methodological protocols and predetermined truth-conditions are displaced, and attention is focused on the way we use language in making our way about, always recognizing that whatever is at issue might be articulated from another perspective using another grammar and that another way of telling the story might elicit a believing tendency that previously was absent. Rather than seeking formal proofs and hard-knobbed signifieds, one attests to what language permits one to say.

Among the proponents of the later Wittgenstein's contribution to the linguistic turn, Stanley Cavell has been particularly helpful in illu-

15. Claude Lévi-Strauss, *The Savage Mind* (Chicago: University of Chicago Press, 1966), 247.

minating how the strategy of linguistic analysis circumvents the epistemological foundationalism that would have us front-load criteria for epistemic justification. He shows, almost effortlessly, how criteria can be liberated from their subservience to the tables of judgment in the classical theory of knowledge. Criteria are refigured against the backdrop of a rhetorical transaction and redesigned to retain their liaison with the ordinary usages in the multiple language-games that make up our sundry forms of life. Appeals to pregiven rules of method and unimpeachable truth-conditions are undermined, and we are advised to exercise a discernment of the everyday circumstances in which we show that something "consists in" or "counts as" something. We will then be able to see, after the theoretical-epistemological dust settles, that what is at issue is "just the ordinary rhetorical structure of the ordinary word 'criterion.' "[16]

The contribution of ordinary language analysis to an understanding of religious discourse has been considerable in both contemporary philosophy of religion and theology. Its main contribution in this arena may well have been to show how easily we become bamboozled in talking about God. And in this linguistic turn, accentuating the close connection between speaking and meaning, language and truth, ordinary language philosophy became a somewhat unexpected legacy of the negative theology of Pseudo-Dionysius, who in *On Divine Names* had already alerted us of the difficulty of saying what God is without taking recourse to saying what he is not. British philosopher of religion and theologian Ian T. Ramsey has examined some of the more telling implications of ordinary language philosophy for theological discourse. He has given particular attention to the linguistic quandaries that arise in the naming of God, revisiting many of the concerns of the fifth-century philosopher and theologian Pseudo-Dionysius. Ramsey examines the logical idiosyncrasies and oddities in the language of prophecy, apocalypticism, miracles, and divine revelation, showing how the choice of theological words and phrases in elucidating the phenomena at issue discloses what he calls "a characteristically religious situation." His description of the religious situation provides a fine illustration of what Wittgenstein apparently had in mind when he spoke of the different "forms of life."[17]

In this progression from the question about God within an epistemological paradigm, to a dismissal of the question by structuralism, and then to a reformulation of the question within ordinary language, there

16. Stanley Cavell, *The Claim of Reason: Wittgenstein: Skepticism, Morality, and Tragedy* (New York: Oxford University Press, 1979), 7–8.

17. Ian T. Ramsey, *Religious Language: An Empirical Placing of Theological Phrases* (New York: Macmillan, 1963), 24–30.

are clearly important shifts and transitions. What is learned from these shifts and transitions, however, is that God-talk is a language game that exhibits certain linguistic oddities. What is the appropriate grammar to use in our references and significations as they pertain to the Deity? This is clearly a decisive and unavoidable question. And it is a question that needs to be radicalized to the point of problematizing the concept of God as a being to whom reference, in whatever sense, can be made, and to whom a bundle of attributes can be assigned. Both the epistemological and the linguistic turn in the specialized discipline of philosophy of religion continued to make purchases upon the concept of God in classical theism. Might it be that a more aggressive confrontation with the theistic construal of the concept of the Deity needs to be maneuvered, possibly with the help of certain insights and inscriptions in the margins of the philosophical tradition from the Greeks onward?

Language, Being, and God

The linguistic turn in philosophy, illustrated in the couplings of language and logic, semantics and semiotics, speaking and ordinary language, and hermeneutics and the linguisticality of being, had some far-reaching consequences for the question about God. It set the requirement for giving studied attention to what is at issue in the grammar of God-talk. In our academies and in our daily transactions we encounter discourse about that which is considered to be divine, sacred, or holy. What resources of language are available to enable us to speak properly about the subject matter at issue? Is there a grammar that might yield positive descriptions about the reality of the divine? Or are we to remain content with the admonition of negative theology that we do well to stick with saying what God is not?

   In this final section of chapter 1, we will investigate some possible approaches to these questions by tracking the fallout of inquiries into the entwinement of language, being, and God. Given the heavy traffic between the corridors of philosophy and theology in the history of metaphysics, it was inevitable that the linguistic turn would mandate a refiguration of the coupling of the problem of being and the question about God against the backdrop of the forms and functions of language.

   It is well known that Heidegger had much to do with setting the agenda on the relation of language and being. However, the path that Heidegger followed in setting this agenda was not all that smooth. And the bearing of the question about God upon Heidegger's sojourns along this path is particularly perplexing. It is important we keep in mind that Heidegger's inquiry standpoint with respect to the issues at stake was not a seamless tapestry. It exhibited various hermeneutical twists and turns, most notably the turn (*Kehre*) from the problem of the "meaning of Being" (*Sinn des Seins*) to the problem of the "truth of Being" (*Wahrheit des Seins*) and then the turn to the "erasure of Being" (*kreuzweise Durchstreichung*). We need, however, to be careful not to construe these different hermeneutical perspectives along the lines of a genealogical development of stages, whereby through the advance from the one to the other the latter is somehow invalidated. They are rather to be understood as intercalating possibilities of thought concerning the issue of Being.

The philosophical task defined as a quest for the meaning of Being unfolds within ruminations on the celebrated ontological/ontic difference, requiring us to be attentive to the all important distinction between Being (*Sein*) and beings (*Seiendes*). According to Heidegger, it is the preoccupation—and virtual obsession—with the latter that has determined the inquiries of metaphysics from the Greeks onward. In the process, the meaning of Being, which putatively informs all particular beings in their multiple relationships, has remained occluded. This is the story of the "forgottenness of Being" (*Vergessenheit des Seins*) that Heidegger is disposed to tell. Only after we have understood why and how the meaning of Being has been forgotten will we be in a position to tell the story of how the forgotten meaning can be retrieved. Somewhere at the center of Heidegger's project of the retrieval/reclamation of the meaning of Being is the emancipation of the descriptive power of non-objectivating "existentials" (*Existenzialen*) from the objectivating categories in the language of metaphysics.

But how does the question about God play itself out in this retrieval of the meaning of Being? How does the grammar about the divine and the holy function within the folds of the ontological/ontic difference? In his work, *Identity and Difference*, Heidegger appears to provide us with a straightforward answer to these questions. "The deity enters into philosophy through the perdurance of which we think at first as the approach to the active nature of the difference between Being and beings." The entrance of the deity into the philosophical lexicon at this juncture, however, appears to be quite ill-fated, for "the perdurance results in and gives Being as the generative ground . . . the cause as *causa sui*." But in the moment that the deity is construed as an originating causal agent, the path to a religious understanding of the deity is blocked. This may indeed, concludes Heidegger, be "the right name for the god of philosophy"; but unfortunately "man can neither pray nor sacrifice to this god. Before the *causa sui,* man can neither fall to his knees in awe nor can he play music and dance before this god."[18]

It is thus that although the ontological/ontic difference opens up possibilities for reclaiming the meaning of Being, it does little to advance the quest for the meaning of the divine. Hence, one is thus not surprised to find that Heidegger, in approaching the problem of Being from the perspective formulated in *Being and Time* as the project of a fundamental ontology that takes its point of departure from a hermeneutic of *Dasein,* is quite insistent on a rather sharp demarcation of the philosophical from the theological enterprise. "There is no such thing as a Christian philosophy; that is an absolute 'square circle'," he writes in "Phenomenology and Theology." Also there is no such discipline as phenomenological theology, "just as there is no phenomenological mathematics."[19]

Yet, the severance of philosophy and theology is nonetheless never complete. Philosophy as fundamental ontology does provide a service of sorts for theological reflection. Ontological analysis with its distinctive existentials provides a conceptual clarification of the structures of human existence that grounds all concrete and ontic self-understanding, including the sojourn of religious faith. "All theological concepts," writes Heidegger, "necessarily contain that understanding of Being which is constitutive of human Dasein, insofar as it exists at all." The example Heidegger provides is that of the universal existential structure of guilt. Guilt, he writes, "functions as a guide for the theological explication of sin."[20] The ontic experience of sin as estrangement or alienation from God receives an ontological understanding of its dynamics through the existential determinant of guilt. So also the life of faith is ontologically comprehended through an analysis of the all encompassing structure of authenticity that drives the economy of *Dasein.* Hence, Heidegger is able to sum up the state of affairs pertaining to the relevance of the ontological and the ontic to religious thought as follows: "Philosophy is the ontological corrective formally pointing out the ontic and, in particular, the pre-Christian content of basic theological concepts."[21]

18. Heidegger, *Identity and Difference,* 71–72.

19. Martin Heidegger, "Phenomenology and Theology," in *The Piety of Thinking,* translation, notes, and commentary, James G. Hart and John C. Maraldo (Bloomington: Indiana University Press, 1976), 21.

20. Ibid.,18–19.

21. Ibid., 20. In a previous volume I developed the thesis that Heidegger's phenomenological ontology as presented in his work, *Being and Time,* can be read as a secularization and ontologization of Søren Kierkegaard's ontic and ethico-religious understanding of human

Moving out from the inquiry standpoint of the ontological/ontic difference, we thus find it possible to address the theological problematic, but only in an oblique and somewhat circuitous manner. At best, ontological analysis can provide a "corrective" for the construction of theological concepts. But it does not get us much further. And there are always the sirens of metaphysics lurking in the background, beckoning us to construe God as a cosmological *causa sui* which explains the origin of beings in their totality. Within such a scheme of inquiry, God functions as a quasi-scientific explanation for the origin of the universe as a totality of beings. This is the destiny of the concept of God in the history of metaphysics, which quite early begins to play itself out as a theo-metaphysics and an onto-theology.

But might it be that God-talk would find a more hospitable environment as one moves from an investigation of the meaning of Being within the folds of the ontological/ontic difference to the question of the truth of Being and the prominence that is accorded to language in the pursuit of this question? In this turning, one finds a switch in vocabulary, away from the cataloguing of the existentials that comprise the structure of *Dasein*'s being-in-the-world, in which language (*Sprache*) is the means for articulating the intelligibility of the existential structures, to a more encompassing role assigned to language as veritably the "house of Being" (*Haus des Seins*). Language becomes the house of Being and upon *Dasein* is conferred the task of serving as the guardian and shepherd of Being (*Hirt des Sein*) rather than striving to become the master of beings (*Herr des Seienden*). Admittedly, the ontological/ontic difference still hovers in the background, but its utility for overcoming the aporia of metaphysics has now run its course.

The spin-off from this hermeneutical shift from meaning to truth and from the ontological/ontic difference to language has certain consequences for the religious question. Truth as "lighting" (*Lichtung*) and "bringing out of hiddenness" (*aletheia*) reminds one of Saint Augustine's doctrine of the *lumen naturale* as the gift from God that makes possible knowledge of his self-disclosure. In this doctrine there is clearly a recollection of a species of Neoplatonic mysticism (which left a permanent impress on Augustine's theology), in which ultimate reality is made accessible directly through a supersensuous apprehension. That some com-

---

existence. One finds very few references to Kierkegaard in Heidegger's writings, and these for the most part are not particularly laudatory. From this one might be led to conclude that Heidegger was more indebted to Kierkegaard than he either realized or was ready to admit. See Calvin O. Schrag, *Existence and Freedom: Towards an Ontology of Human Finitude* (Evanston: Northwestern University Press, 1961).

mentators on the thought of Heidegger pursued this line, ascribing to
Heidegger a "mysticism of Being" (*Seinsmystik*), is well known. Although
Heidegger may indeed have opened up such a route, he did not follow
it, because he was fully cognizant that mysticism as a theological mode of
knowing continues to reside in the metaphysical. However, a linkage of
philosophical inquiry and religious thought continues in its attenuated
form even in this turning to the truth of Being. In his "Letter on Humanism," which provides the most explicit statement on the new terrain
explored in Heidegger II, we are told the following: "Only from the truth
of Being can the essence of the holy be thought. Only from the essence
of the holy can the essence of divinity be thought. Only in the light of
the essence of divinity can it be thought and said what the word 'God' is
to signify."[22]

It is in the shift to Heidegger III, occasioned by the second *Kehre*,
which can properly be understood as a radicalization of the first *Kehre*,
in which the question about God undergoes its most intense reconfigu-
ration. That which guides the inquiry in Heidegger III is the shift from
the grammar of Being to that of the "event of appropriation" (*Ereignis*),
and a refiguration of language into the performativity of "saying" (*Sagen*)
as expressive of poetic thinking and dwelling. As a result of this eventful
turning, Being undergoes an erasure, a "crossing out" (*kreuzeweise Durchstreichung*), which heralds the appropriation of a concernful dwelling
that is beyond and otherwise than Being.[23]

Here the Being-problem, both within the folds of the ontologi-
cal/ontic difference and as an inquiry into the truth of Being as language, would appear to be decisively overcome. Within this new space
of poetic thinking and dwelling, the question about God directs us to a
region that is otherwise than Being. The question about God is reposi-
tioned not only on the hither side of inquiries into the totality of being
and a possible highest kind of being, that is, within a metaphysics of theism, but also on the hither side of the *Seinsfrage* itself. Now there is still a
"saying," the narration of a saga, the telling of a story of our caring for the
earth, our sojourn as mortals, and our experience of divinities. But this
saying is no longer that of the language of theology. Indeed, it is the grammar of an atheology. It has to do with a commemorating rather than with
a representing, a showing rather than a referring, a setting forth through
narrative rather than an explaining via philosophical discourse. It is a
saying that furrows a path not only beyond metaphysics and epistemology

22. Heidegger, "Letter on Humanism," 253.
23. See particularly Martin Heidegger, *Zur Seinsfrage* (Frankfurt: Vittorio Klostermann,
1956), 30–35.

but also beyond theology. There is still a point to the God-question, but it needs to be asked in a new way; and in asking it, Heidegger finds himself talking about earth and sky, divinities and mortals—quite analogous, one might say, to Nietzsche's remark about Thales. After having seen the unity of all that is, Thales sought to communicate it and found himself talking of water![24]

Our brief excursus on the hermeneutical shifts in Heidegger's interrogation of the issues of Being and language has been designed as a thought experiment of thinking with, and sometimes against, him in an effort to re-ask and reconfigure the question about God. In doing so, we admittedly may have done some violence to his texts; but we submit that we have remained quite "Heideggerian" in doing so, recalling his admonition in *Kant and the Problem of Metaphysics* that in dealing with Kant's corpus of writings "in order to wrest from the actual words that which these words 'intend to say', every interpretation must necessarily resort to violence."[25] We can surely assume that what works in Heidegger's take on Kant ought also work in our thinking with Heidegger beyond Heidegger![26]

The pivotal juncture in our path of rethinking the question about God, with and against Heidegger, is the transition "beyond theology," beyond not only the grammar of onto-theology as defined in the history of metaphysics but also beyond the grammar of fundamental ontology and the problem of Being itself. In pursuing this path of rethinking, we will need to remember the importance accorded to language by representatives of the linguistic turn as maneuvered both by the ordinary language school and by latter day hermeneuticists and deconstructionists

24. Friedrich Nietzsche, *Philosophy in the Tragic Age of the Greeks*, trans. Marianne Cowan (Chicago: Henry Regnery, 1962), 45. It is important that we not interpret Heidegger's narrative about earth and sky, and divinities and mortals, as an overture to a theological treatise. What is at issue here is poetical disclosure rather than theological discourse. Heidegger underscored this point in his response to queries about his use of the grammar of "divinity" and the "holy" in his "Letter on Humanism": "With respect to the text referred to from the 'Letter on Humanism,' what is being discussed there is the God of the poet, not the revealed God. There is mentioned merely what philosophical thinking is capable of on its own. Whether this may also be of significance for theology cannot be said because there is for us no third case by which it could be decided," Heidegger, "Appendix: Conversation with Martin Heidegger, Recorded by Hermann Noack," in *The Piety of Thinking*, 65.

25. Martin Heidegger, *Kant and the Problem of Metaphysics*, trans. James S. Churchill (Bloomington: Indiana University Press, 1962), 207.

26. For an extended discussion by the author of Heidegger's two turnings, which may well contain a "resort to violence" of the kind that Heidegger resorts to in his interpretation of Kant, see Calvin O. Schrag, "The Three Heideggers," in *Philosophical Papers: Betwixt and Between* (Albany: State University of New York Press, 1994), 159–73.

who have highlighted the revelatory function of poetic thinking and given prominence to the role of narrative. In the end this may lead us to a sustained consideration of the resources of narration in our efforts to think beyond the stultifying categories of traditional metaphysics and the hyperspecialized and discipline-specific vocabulary that has traveled with these categories, enabling us to speak of narrative as the culmination of the linguistic turn in recent thought. We will need to tap the resources of storytelling, in which there is much ado about speaking and hearing, saying and the said, in hopes that these resources may open doors and windows to what resides beyond the thought and the language that hitherto has made inflated purchases on metaphysical, ontological, and theological enterprises.

In our efforts to think beyond the stock categories and sedimented grammar of traditional modes of philosophical and theological thought, we are not striking out on our own. We are aided by the likes of Paul Tillich, Emmanuel Levinas, Jean-Luc Marion, and Jacques Derrida, who with their provocative notions of "theism transcended," "otherwise than being," "God without being," and "religion without religion" have oriented us into what may be promising directions. From time to time in the text that follows, the contributions of these contemporary thinkers, who have aided us in the framing of our project, will need to be critically addressed.

It will be necessary to experiment with different ways of saying what can be said about that which resides on the hither side of the "beyond" when we make the move beyond theology. Heidegger taught us the ways of deconstruction so that we could move "beyond metaphysics." Since the publication of Richard Rorty's *Philosophy and the Mirror of Nature* we have been enjoined to proceed "beyond epistemology."[27] Now we are entertaining a move "beyond theology." What it is that resides on the fringes of these beyonds—if indeed anything!—is not that clear. To be sure, we are informed by Rorty that his move beyond epistemology opens a route to hermeneutics. The end of epistemology heralds the beginning of hermeneutical discourse. But we soon learn that for Rorty hermeneutics supplies basically a "negative" function, playing itself out in the conversation of humankind as a hermeneutics of suspicion, bent upon an undermining of any and all foundationalist claims. But this hermeneutics of suspicion is for Rorty through and through "reactive." It reacts against the epistemological illusion that an accurate representation of reality

---

27. Richard Rorty, *Philosophy and the Mirror of Nature* (Princeton, N.J.: Princeton University Press, 1979). See particularly pt. 3, chap. 7, "From Epistemology to Hermeneutics," 315–56.

is possible. At best, this leaves us with a "negative epistemology," which might find some species of an analog in the negative theology of certain fourth- and fifth-century theologians.

It is thus that further attention needs to be given to discourse about the beyond—be it the beyond of metaphysics, the beyond of epistemology, or the beyond of theology. Are there any positive features, characteristics, or determinations that can be ascribed to the "beyond" of theology, the "transcendence" of theism, and the "otherwise" than being; or are these indexicals simply indicative of that which is just utterly, totally, and unqualifiedly beyond, transcendent, or otherwise? If so, the *topos-utopos* in which they reside is outside any solicitations within language and discourse. Does the move beyond exhibit any recursivity to that from which the movement to the beyond proceeds, any resources for delimiting the economies of epistemology, metaphysics, and theology, at once relativizing their conceptual constructions and providing a sheet anchor against their idolatric tendencies? Is the beyond of theology in any way a pointer to an "aneconomic" dynamic, no longer beholden to the metaphors of production and exchange, distribution and consumption, where the issues at stake involve the control and management of knowledge, being, or God? Does the move beyond, the quest for transcendence, the acknowledgment of that which is otherwise, in some manner yield a new way to talk about knowledge, about being, and about God?

2

Beyond Theism and Atheism

The Concept of God after Postmodernity

The difficulties that beset one in defining the distinguishing features of postmodernity are well known. And these difficulties are compounded when one brings the concept of God into the mix. If postmodernism is to be understood as "incredulity toward metanarratives," as Jean-François Lyotard would have it, then it would seem that any question about God would be ruled out from the start. Surely a narrative about the Deity gathers considerable breadth and depth. Such would allegedly be a story that explains the whence and wherefore of all that is, and the tale as told by the metaphysics of theism would appear to be precisely of this kind.

But it is not all that easy to sort out the defining marks of theism. The history of philosophy and religion, both in the East and in the West, has provided us with a colorful variety of senses that at different times have become attached to the term. And when one finally arrives at the point where one is ready to lay down a definition, one quickly realizes that necessary qualifications are required. Defining *theism* is indeed a formidable task; yet, some clarity on the use of the term needs to be achieved. And if we cannot get clear on the meaning of *theism,* then the meaning of *atheism* will elude us as well. Plainly enough, both theism and atheism involve discourse about *theos,* which we commonly translate as "God." Theists are motivated to make claims that God exists; atheists are convinced that God does not exist; and then there are the philosophical middle-of-the-roaders, the charitable skeptics, who find the issue to be quite undecidable.

The position-taking on the question as to the existence or nonexistence of God becomes even more fuzzy and elusive when the issue of the *nature* of God, whose existence has been either affirmed or denied, arises. This is clearly an issue that needs to be addressed if the very concept of God is to avoid becoming the proverbial slippery eel that forever eludes our grasp. Apparently not just anything can qualify as the referent in

God-talk. There must be some distinguishing features that characterize what the learned and the vulgar alike have been wont to call God. These distinguishing features, however, are most difficult to pin down. Hence, one needs, time and again, to strive for maximum clarity in the use of the term that provides the lynchpin for theistic belief and practice.

The sundry attempts at consolidating the meaning of the word *God* via dictionary and encyclopedia definitions are instructive for highlighting both the advantages and disadvantages of such a project. Such is the case, for example, in the entry "Theism" in the monumental eight-volume *Encyclopedia of Philosophy*, where we read: "Theism signifies belief in one God (*theos*) who is (a) personal, (b) worthy of adoration, and (c) separate from the world but (d) continuously active in it."[1] With the proper amendments, this could be useful as a working definition designed to get the conversation going. Theism is a belief system in which knowledge claims are made about the existence and the nature of *theos*. In the standard expressions of theism, particularly in Western religions, the beliefs at issue involve claims that there is *at least* one God; and in the monotheism of Judaic, Christian, and Islamic theology, one finds adamant claims that there is one God *only*.

If, however, we are to recognize polytheistic and henotheistic beliefs as representative of theism as well, then of course the definition will have to be expanded to allow for some multiplicity in the divine realm. The characterization of the Deity (or deities) as personal, as stipulated by the encyclopedia definition, would appear to apply to most persuasions of theism, but again certain exceptions would need to be acknowledged, particularly in Eastern philosophy and religion. The characterization of theism as involving a concept of *theos* "worthy of adoration" is also instructive. In the varieties of theism, God is commonly characterized as "sacred" and "holy," requiring respectful allegiance and sustained obedience. The remaining two characterizations, *theos* as "separate from the world" and "continuously active in it," may constitute the main problem for a general definition of theism. Rigid adherence to these defining marks would exclude in one stroke both pantheism and deism, which terminologically at any rate qualify as varieties of theism.

Our brief analysis of this particular encyclopedic characterization of theism has brought to light the extraordinary difficulty in landing upon a definition of theism modeled after a class concept in set theory that would include all of its members. It does not appear that one is able

---

1. *Encyclopedia of Philosophy*, vol. 8, editor in chief Paul Edwards (New York: Macmillan, 1967), 97.

to devise a definition of theism that supplies the requisite universality to enable one to identify all of its particular expressions. Nonetheless, if we are to incorporate God-talk into our discourse, we need in some manner to take up the slack in its varied usage. In the history of theism it has been primarily metaphysics that has lent its services, either explicitly or implicitly, for achieving such a consolidation. God as the proper object of belief is a being about whom existence claims can be made and whose nature can be described by certain identifying features. Eternality, immutability, self-subsistent or nondependent existence, and supreme perfection have been the most common metaphysical attributes ascribed to the Deity. Onto these have been grafted the more distinctly religious signifiers such as Lord, Judge, and Redeemer. In dealing with the issue of the relation of God to the world, theists have found the metaphysical categories of cause and effect and the theological distinction between Creator and creation to be particularly helpful.

It is thus we are able to understand how theism would become a candidate for a metanarrative bent upon totalization, as defined by the spokespersons for postmodernism. Other examples of metanarratives identified by postmodern thinkers include dialectical idealism, Enlightenment rationality, historical materialism, and capitalism.[2] A metanarrative, in the thought of postmodernity, is a totalizing narrative, designed to encompass explanations of origins and ends. The narrative about God within the varieties of theistic metaphysics has the markings of such a totalizing narrative. It is a story of how the totality of beings exhibits an intelligibility and a unity by virtue of the causal efficacy of a supernatural being who remains uncaused. God as infinite and supremely perfect being is a veritable *ens causa sui* that provides an explanation for the totality of all finite beings but remains immune to any request for an explanation of its own existence. The story of theism is a story about an origin and an end, a genealogy and a teleology, an alpha and an omega. As a cosmology, such a narrative about the Deity quickly translates into a metascientific account of the beginnings of the universe and the emergence of life on the planet. As a history of humankind, it becomes an account of God as the Lord of history and the panorama of human events as a *Heilsgeschichte,* a "history of salvation." In this totalizing function, both on the cosmic

2. See particularly Jean-François Lyotard, *The Postmodern Condition: A Report on Knowledge,* trans. Geoff Bennington and Brian Massumi (Minneapolis: University of Minnesota Press, 1984), where he writes: "I will use the term *modern* to designate any science that legitimates itself with reference to a metadiscourse of this kind making an explicit appeal to some grand narrative, such as the dialectics of Spirit, the hermeneutics of meaning, the emancipation of the rational or working subject, or the creation of wealth," xxiii.

and the historical plane, the story about the ways of the Deity (or deities) quickly becomes a grand narrative.

This may well explain why the death of God theme has solicited so much interest in the postmodern literature, saturated as it is with censures of metanarratives and attacks on claims for unity and totality. The postmodern ethos would have us opt for local narratives (*petit recits*) and be done with quests for unification and totalization as we busy ourselves with a celebration of difference and multiplicity, heterogeneity and paralogy. It is thus any effort to address the question about God after postmodernity will need to take into account the postmodern challenge on these issues. It will need to give studied attention to how the concept of God figures in religious narratives and how a new perspective might be taken on the relevance of unity and totality in religious discourse.

In conjunction with squaring God-talk with the constraints of narrativity, addressing the postmodern challenge on the issue requires giving attention to the modernity-versus-postmodernity problematic. There appears to be some consensus that the relation of the postmodern to the modern is not one of simple chronological development. Postmodernity is not something that *comes after* modernity, chronologically speaking. Lyotard has made this point quite clear: "Postmodernism thus understood is not modernism at its end but in the nascent state, and this state is constant."[3] However, what particular connection obtains between the two and how the one might envelop the other remains somewhat indeterminate.

A possible approach to the cross-reading of modernity and postmodernity as it relates to the inquiry into the concept of the Deity would be to move out from Max Weber's well-known definition of the modernity problematic as having to do with the "stubborn differentiation" of the three culture-spheres of science, morality, and art. This differentiation, and its alleged unfortunate consequences, has both cultural and philosophical roots. Immanuel Kant is commonly credited with having provided the philosophical format in which the spheres of science, morality, and art fall out as split off from each other. Although one can find in his three critiques overtures toward a unification of the three spheres, it is generally conceded that his efforts along these lines failed and that it was left to Hegel to reconfigure the project of unification. Now whether Hegel succeeded where Kant came up short remains one of those issues on which future treatises will continue to be written.

The postmodern response to this alleged problem of modernity turns basically on a jettisoning of the quest for unification that defines the

3. Ibid, 79.

state of affairs as a problem to begin with. Neither Kant nor Hegel, proclaim the postmodernists, need be taken all that seriously. Kant should not be taken that seriously in his division of scientific, ethical, and aesthetic discourse in the first place; and Hegel should not be taken that seriously for fashioning an ontology of identity wherewith to solve a problem that is more artificial than real. Why not simply embrace the heterogeneity of the three culture-spheres and acknowledge different prevailing discourses within each of them? Such is the response offered by postmodernity, and it is a response informed at once by Lyotard's call for a heterogeneity of language games, Foucault's pluralization of microsocial practices, Deleuze and Guattari's appeal to the multiplicity of the rhizomatic over against the unity of the arborescent, and Derrida's privileging of *différance* over sameness and presence. On this particular issue, admittedly one of a very few, it would seem that postmodernists speak with a single voice.

Jürgen Habermas's response to the postmodern indictment of the contributions of modernity is at once singular and instructive. His long-term goal is to rescue the "discourse of modernity" from the "counterdiscourse of postmodernity" in such a manner that the contributions of both Kant and Hegel can be salvaged. Unlike his postmodern critics, Habermas is of the mind that the issue posed by Kant in regard to the topography of the three culture-spheres of science, morality, and art, is indeed a *genuine* issue. To be sure, Kant's transcendental philosophy lacked the resources to solve the resultant splitting apart of the three spheres, but Hegel had the right idea about how to deal with this problem. In his early period, that of his Jena writings, Hegel was still on the right track. He had at his disposal a vibrant notion of community wherewith to ground his concept of rationality. But he then took a wrong turn in his later philosophy in which he sought to unify the differentiated culture-spheres with an appeal to a subject-centered reason and unsupportable claims as to what such a rationality in the guise of absolute knowledge might accomplish.[4]

In this rescue effort on the part of Habermas to reinstall the discourse of modernity, albeit not in an uncritical fashion, Foucault and Derrida in particular come under attack. Foucault is faulted for his inability to bring his genealogical method into synch with viable projects of normative ethics and social criticism. Indeed, according to Habermas,

---

4. Jürgen Habermas, *The Philosophical Discourse of Modernity: Twelve Lectures,* trans. Frederick Lawrence (Cambridge, Mass.: MIT Press, 1987), 40, 80.

any move toward a normative ethics ultimately remains blocked. Given his preoccupation with the genealogy of power relations in personal and social existence, Foucault is unable to deliver any ethical norms and directives for social reform. Proceeding from what Habermas calls Foucault's "ascetic description of kaleidoscopically changing practices of power," the most that his genealogical historiography can provide is a "presentistic, relativistic, cryptonormative illusory science."[5]

Although Habermas's critique of Foucault may be somewhat over-drawn, the problem of uniting a genealogy of power with normative considerations would appear to remain an unsolved problem for Foucault. Habermas's attack on Derrida is equally strident and unrelenting. Derrida is chided for leveling the distinctions that mark differences of content across the spectrum of science, philosophy, and literature. And in doing so, Habermas claims Derrida confuses "world-disclosing" strategies with "problem-solving" modes of thought. Literature and art are well suited to accomplish the former; science and philosophy are better equipped to do the latter. Derrida, according to Habermas, levels these distinctions of genre and function "in order to equate philosophy with literature and criticism. He fails to recognize the special status that both philosophy and literary criticism, each in its own way, assume as mediators between expert cultures and the everyday world."[6]

Like Habermas's assault on the thought of Foucault, his broadside against Derrida's project strikes us as excessively harsh. We are disposed to be somewhat more charitable in recognizing the contributions of Foucault and Derrida and the proponents of postmodernity more generally in calling the world's attention to the phenomena of multiplicity, heterogeneity, and difference in both our personal and social existence. Yet, one does well—and here one can certainly learn something from Habermas—to proceed with some caution before submitting an unqualified endorsement of the postmodern philosophical program. It will be important to give some attention to what sort of unity, identity, and totality come under indictment in the postmodernists' disputation with modernity. Are unity, identity, and totality in every sense to be ruled out of court, or may there be some sustainable notions of what identifies, unifies, and totalizes? Also, some of the sliddery grammar in the postmodernist vocabulary requires critical attention, and the facile slide from

5. Ibid., 275–76.
6. Ibid., 207.

multiplicity to heterogeneity and from difference to paralogy needs in particular to be given careful scrutiny.[7]

That there are multiple vocabularies in play in the discourses of science, morality, and art that allow, or even require, making careful distinctions between the language in each of the spheres certainly needs to be acknowledged. But whether this multiplicity and difference translates into heterogeneity and incommensurability is quite another matter. Differences in discourse about the behavior of matter, about moral obligations, and about aesthetic sensibilities do not add up to a heterogeneity that would foreclose any communication *within* the regions of the three discourses nor *across* them. One may indeed be done with the traditional metaphysically front-loaded concepts of identity, unity, and totality and still find a space for communication both within and across the culture-spheres of science, morality, and art. As I have argued in previous works, there are resources for surmounting the unacceptable dichotomies of heterogeneity and unity, difference and identity, particularity and universality. These resources reside in the dynamics of a "transversal" rationality, enabling a communication that is able to move across the landscape of differences without coming to rest in a hegemonic unity. I have called such communication "transversal communication."[8]

The merit in the use of the concept of transversality in this characterization of rationality and communication resides in its potential for multidisciplinary investigations. It is a concept that does duty in mathematics, the physical sciences, the life sciences, the social sciences, philosophy, and literature. In topology, transversality functions as a generalization of orthogonality; in particle-theory physics, transverse mass complements the notion of longitudinal mass; in physiology, the concept is used to describe the entwinement of fibers; in anatomy, it depicts the alignment of vertebrae; in the social sciences, the term has been employed to describe the workings of institutional organizations; in philosophy, the concept has been used to illustrate the structure and dynamics of consciousness; and in literature, it has been called upon to explain narrative form and function.

Across the various disciplines, the concept of transversality exhibits the interrelated senses of lying across, extending over, contact without

7. For an extended discussion of these and related issues in the corpus of the postmodern literature, see Calvin O. Schrag, *The Resources of Rationality: A Response to the Postmodern Challenge* (Bloomington: Indiana University Press, 1992).

8. See particularly chap. 6, "Transversal Rationality," in ibid.,148–79, and chap. 4, "The Self in Transcendence," in Calvin O. Schrag, *The Self after Postmodernity* (New Haven, Conn.: Yale University Press, 1997), 110–48.

absorption, convergence without coincidence, and unity without strict identity. This play of meaning allows one to speak of commonalities and conjunctions that do not violate the integrity of differences. Recognizing that scientific description and explanation, ethical prescription and evaluation, and aesthetic evocation and appreciation entail distinctions with a genuine difference, one can nonetheless speak of legitimation and appeals to reason in each, on the basis of which communication across the putative divides becomes possible. One can give reasons for the truth of propositions, right actions, and good art without having the criteria of judgment in each of the spheres becoming coincident with one or the other. Rationality, of a somewhat broader stripe to be sure than the strict criteriology of modern epistemology would allow, is able to move across the space of each. And it is this broader notion of rationality linked with communication that provides a sheet anchor against the presumption of absolute knowledge by any one of the culture-spheres, be it science, morality, or art.

Matters do, however, become more complicated when religious discourse is brought into the mix with the scientific, the moral, and the aesthetic. On this issue, neither the framers of modernity nor the reformers of postmodernity have been all that helpful. It was modernity that produced the mindset of the Enlightenment with its rejection of the tradition, particularly those aspects of the tradition that involved religious beliefs and practices. God was written off as an unnecessary principle of explanation. "We have no need of such a hypothesis," wrote Pierre Simon Laplace, consolidating the Enlightenment view on matters theological. Clearly in the background of this uncharitable view of religion as a legitimate culture-sphere was the modern epistemological criteriology, modeled after the natural sciences, which ruled out of court any knowledge that fell short of objective validation. The postmodern approach to the issue of religion is not that of modernity, for postmodernism will have little truck with the modern epistemological paradigm. But frightened as postmodernists are by metanarratives, they too are unable to find a comfortable place for religious discourse. Whether as the first and final cause of the universe or as the lord of history, God is a unity rather than a multiplicity, one and the same for all eternity, accounting for both the existence and the design of the totality of finite entities. And this for the postmodernist does indeed add up to a grand narrative.

It soon becomes evident that the use and abuse of narrative is very much in the eye of the storm that has occasioned the postmodern challenge. This challenge not only is placed at the door of philosophy of religion and theology but veritably moves across the disciplinary divides of academe. Postmodern literature, postmodern education, postmodern science, postmodern culture studies, postmodern politics, postmodern philosophy, postmodern theology—and the list need not stop here—all have to do with lessons that can be learned from the ways of narrative. The literature on narrative itself is burgeoning, providing the wider public, both inside and outside the academy, with multiple narratives about narrative, discussions of various types of narratives, specific and more general uses of narrative, weaker and stronger versions of signification at play in the semantics of narration.

Narrative is becoming a much discussed topic in recent psychological and social science as well as in the rapidly developing field of cognitive science. Donald Polkinghorne, a theorist and practitioner in the field of psychiatry, has given narrative a prominent place in his discipline. He sees narrative as a "form of meaning making" that plays a cognitive role in human self-understanding. As it relates to his discipline, he is particularly interested in the contribution narrative might make in the design of research strategies in which one uses narratives to help patients understand themselves and the human world in which they exist.[9] A related use of narrative in the interest of self-understanding is found in Mark Johnson's tracing of certain implications of cognitive science for ethics. Like Polkinghorne, Johnson comes down heavy on the cognitive role of narrative. Narrative, avers Johnson, is more than a literary exercise. It is a way of understanding ourselves and the world we inhabit. "Narrative is not just an explanatory device, but is actually constitutive of the way we experience things."[10]

The most ambitious use of narrative to date for philosophical inquiry can be found in Paul Ricoeur's three-volume work *Time and Narrative*. The formidable task Ricoeur sets for himself in this extended discussion is that of taming the aporia that results from the bifurcation of cosmological-metaphysical and existential-phenomenological time. On the one hand, we have the objectively measured time of the clock and the calendar, metaphysically dissected into a serial progression of instants; on the other hand, we are apprised of experienced or lived time, holistic and qualitative in character, elucidated by way of phenomenological description. The tension between these two forms of time has posed a recalcitrant problem since the time of the Greeks. Ricoeur revisits this problem, working out from the texts of Aristotle. He teases out of Aristotle's definition of plot a reconfigured notion of emplotment, which

9. See particularly Donald Polkinghorne, *Narrative Knowing and the Human Sciences* (Albany: State University of New York Press, 1988).

10. Mark Johnson, *Moral Imagination: Implications of Cognitive Science for Ethics* (Chicago: University of Chicago Press, 1993), 11.

he then cross-reads with Augustine's reflections on the time of human consciousness. From this comparative and creative reinterpretation of Aristotle and Augustine, a way is paved to the uses of narrative in an understanding of human and historical time in such a manner as to have it intersect with the time of the cosmos.[11]

J. Wentzel van Huyssteen in his various writings has given particular attention to the impact of postmodern narrativity on the disciplines of science and theology in particular, addressing some of the problems that arise as the result of the breakdown of communication between the two disciplines. Postmodern science, enamored with shifting paradigms, instabilities, unpredictability, and incommensurability, will have little truck with grand narratives as vehicles for the legitimation of scientific knowledge. Scientific knowledge is legitimated within local contexts of inquiry. In recognition of the inescapable pluralism of competing and contradictory theories, paradigms, and research programs, scientific inquiry exhibits a profound skepticism with regard to universal criteria and norms that in the past have been appealed to in guiding scientific investigations. What this amounts to on the epistemological side of the ledger, according to van Huyssteen, is *the turn from foundationalism to holism.*[12] We must be careful, however, not to construe this holism that replaces foundationalism with the holism of world-view philosophizing. It is a holism that remains rooted in the local social practices of interpreting past scientific work and setting agenda for future research.

Admittedly, the postmodern emphasis on local narratives and the diversity of language games and social practices makes a contribution in its own right. Yet, there are, van Huyssteen reminds us, some trouble spots along the way: "In a postmodern world, however, which has been fragmented into a collage of many isolated worlds that cannot be unified by any 'grand' narrative, what is to become of science, philosophy, and any possible philosophy of science? . . . In this postmodern space where science displays its own diversity and plurality, there seems to be little room for the philosopher of science to initiate a metadiscourse for elucidating what is going on in science, or what the rationality of science should be about."[13]

11. See Paul Ricoeur, *Time and Narrative,* vols. 1 and 2, trans. Kathleen McLaughlin and David Pellauer; vol. 3, trans. Kathleen Blamey and David Pellauer (Chicago: University of Chicago Press, 1985–88). See also Schrag, *The Resources of Rationality,* particularly chap. 4, "Narrative and the Claims of Reason," 90–115.

12. J. Wentzel van Huyssteen, "Is There a Postmodern Challenge in Theology and Science?," in *Essays in Postfoundationalist Theology* (Grand Rapids, Mich.: W. B. Eerdmans, 1997), 267.

13. Ibid., 271.

As one probes the contentions in the postmodern challenge, it soon becomes evident that the issue of rationality emerges as the principal bone of contention. How does it stand with rationality in the saga of scientific discovery and in the multiple research programs? Upon further inquiry we find that it is precisely the postmodern assault on the resources of reason that also concerns the theologian. J. Wentzel van Huyssteen's statement on the issue is succinct and to the point: "One of the most crucial challenges for theology and science today can therefore be stated as follows: Can we successfully deal with the problem of the shaping of rationality, and thereby also identify the epistemic and nonepistemic values that shape religious and scientific reflection within a postmodern context?"[14]

The issue of rationality becomes particularly acute when one is confronted with the request to clarify the uses of reason in narratives about the Deity or deities and how such might maintain commerce with the world of nature and history. Is it possible to fashion narratives about God that do not resort to problematic epistemological claims and make heavy purchases on the totalizing narratives of theo-metaphysics? It surely is no accident that the concept of God that Enlightenment thinkers found so repugnant, as well as that which functions as the quintessential exemplar of identity and unity in the postmodern version of metanarratives, very much resembled the portrait of God in classical theistic metaphysics. And it was Nietzsche, commonly credited with having been the first postmodernist of note, who had the courage to proclaim that the God of classical theism, whose portrait had been touched up with a Platonized Christianity, had died. Such a "God," of course, had never lived—except as an invention in the minds of theistically inclined metaphysicians and mainstream Christian theologians, who were quick to adopt a metaphysical strategy for doing theology. To be sure, the consequences of this proclamation of the death of God may in the end have profoundly baffled Nietzsche himself, but in a somewhat serendipitous fashion he forced us to ask the question, How does it stand with the concept of the Deity after postmodernity? Might it be that in pursuit of this question we will be led, in the words of van Huyssteen, "to the point where we can celebrate the truth behind truth, the God behind God, and the religious behind religion"?[15]

14. Ibid., 277. For an extended discussion by J. Wentzel van Huyssteen on the project of developing a postfoundationalist concept of rationality in addressing the relation between science and theology, see his recent work *The Shaping of Rationality: Toward Interdisciplinarity in Theology and Science* (Grand Rapids, Mich.: W. B. Eerdmans, 1999).

15. van Huyssteen, *Essays in Postfoundationalist Theology,* 279.

Reactive Atheism

It would be difficult to find a more puzzling theme in Nietzsche's extensive corpus of writings than that of the death of God. The theme comprises the binding textuality of *Thus Spake Zarathustra, The Gay Science,* and *The Will to Power.* In the former work, the death of the Deity is the paramount message in the Zarathustra narrative. After a ten-year spiritual struggle in solitude, having distanced himself from the crowds of humanity, seeking enlightenment through withdrawal, Zarathustra descends from the mountains and passes through a forest on his way back to the villages. On his way he encounters a saint who offers the gift of song in praise to his god. The saint then asks Zarathustra what it is that he might bring as a gift. To this Zarathustra replies: "What could I have to give you? Let me go quickly lest I take something away from you!" Quietly he then moves on, saying to himself: "Could it be possible? This old saint in the forest hath not heard of this, that *God is dead.*"[16]

That some species of atheism is at issue here would seem to be undeniable. But apparently it is an atheism of a quite idiosyncratic sort. It is an atheism roundly qualified. Nietzsche tells us in *The Antichrist* that what peculiarly defines his thought is not that he rejects the concept of God as such. It is rather that he is unable to attest to the God that Christianity, and more specifically the Apostle Paul, fashioned.[17] For Nietzsche, the God of institutionalized Christianity, what Kierkegaard had called "Christendom," is indeed dead. And on this particular point the similarities between Nietzsche's *The Antichrist* and Kierkegaard's *Attack on "Christendom"* are quite remarkable. The God of institutionalized Christianity is for Nietzsche a veritable *negation* of divinity, a devaluation of all that is noble and life-affirming—and it is of course the church as the vehicle of institutionalized Christianity that is the Antichrist in masquerade.

The death of God theme is thus a reaction against and a rebuke of the concept of God in institutionalized Christianity. But it is more than that. It is also, and at the same time, a negation of the concept of God in theistic metaphysics, to which Christianity appealed in its effort to align Christian theology with Greek philosophy. And there is yet

16. Friedrich Nietzsche, *Thus Spake Zarathustra,* in *The Portable Nietzsche,* trans. and ed. Walter Kaufmann (New York: Viking Press, 1954), 124.

17. "That we find no God—either in history or in nature or behind nature—is not what differentiates *us,* but that we experience what has been revered as God, not as 'godlike' but as miserable, as absurd, as harmful, not merely as an error, but as a *crime against life.* We deny God as God. If one were to *prove* this God of the Christians to us, we should be even less able to believe in him. In a formula: *deus, qualem Paulus creavit, dei negatio,*" *The Antichrist,* in *The Portable Nietzsche,* 267.

more. Insofar as the concept of God in classical theism bought into the "two-world" metaphysics of Plato, it became a contributing factor in the development of nihilism. Plato's invention of his otherworldly forms—eternal, immutable, and perfect—and his devaluation of becoming is understood by Nietzsche as having set the stage for the advent of nihilism. It is on this "other world" that Christianity and Christianized European civilization pinned their hopes, only to have them upended in a profound metaphysical disappointment, inviting the specter of nihilism Nietzsche defined in *The Will to Power* as the predominant threat to the whole of Western culture. The death of God thus functions as a revelation of the conditions for nihilism—a nihilism that itself is to be overcome through a robust self-affirmation of life as life.

Zarathustra's message proclaiming the demise of the Deity assumes significant proportions as it compenetrates the whole corpus of Nietzsche's literary productivity. It is of some moment to note that there is in this message as proclaimed by Zarathustra a co-present puzzling theme—that of the gift. The Gordian notion of the gift is here introduced, a notion that later plays itself out in *Thus Spake Zarathustra* as a pivotal virtue (*die schenkende Tugend*). The old saint in the forest requests of Zarathustra a gift. But Zarathustra is unable to give his gift without taking something away from the recipient. Here we are apprised of an aporia that appears to reside in the very heart of all gift giving and gift receiving, an aporia that has elicited widespread attention in the subsequent literature on the topic from Marcel Mauss to Jacques Derrida. This will need to become a central motif in part 2 in the present study.

The proper name for Nietzsche's atheism—if indeed the term retains any applicability in his scheme of things—is "reactive atheism." And it is a reactive atheism that is able to play itself out as a species of "negative atheology." If not a negation of God in every sense conceivable, which as we have seen is a claim Nietzsche stops short of making, it calls for a negation of the concept of a supernatural being in classical theism as well as a negation of the God of cultural Christianity. The commingling of these two portraits of God has resulted in the concept of an enfeebled deity, called upon to protect those who lack the power to affirm life, falling victim to a herd morality, with its resentment of all things noble. Now whether Nietzsche's idiosyncratic *via negativa* can be appropriated as a path to a positive notion of the Deity, transcending the theism versus atheism problematic itself, as suggested by the fourth- and fifth-century proponents of negative theology, may merit some attention. The difficulty, however, is that of locating a space and a content on the hither side of the concept of God in Western philosophy and theology. There are suggestions of such a possible move in Nietzsche's thought. He is quite positive in his assessment of the original Hebraic concept of God and sees the so-called progression of the concept of God from the "God of Israel" to that of the "Christian God" as a retrogression.[18] The most regrettable error of the Christian concept of God is that it portrays a denatured and enfeebled god, a deity divested of power.

At this juncture it is tempting to fill the space opened by the negation of the Christian-baptized Greek-inspired deity with a new concept of God as the superlative exemplar of the will to power. The will to power in the end becomes Nietzsche's paramount interpretive category, not only in the edited notes that make up *The Will to Power* but already in *Thus Spake Zarathustra*. "Where I found the living, there I found will to power"; avers Zarathustra, "and even in the will of those who serve I found the will to be master. . . . Only where there is life is there also will: not will to life but—thus I teach you—will to power."[19] In the wake of the demise of the enfeebled deity of institutionalized Christianity, it would appear that a space is opened for an epiphany of the will to power, a spiritual élan that pervades the whole of existence, both human and nonhuman, providing the condition for self-affirmation and self-mastery, which in the end is pretty much the long and the short of Nietzsche's much-maligned symbol of the Overman (*Übermensch*). Nietzsche's negative atheology would thus seem to herald a new deity whose name is Power, in whose name the resources for authentic existence become available. In the beginning was Power, Power was with God and Power was God; and Power became flesh and dwells among us! Such indeed appears to be the message according to Nietzsche's Zarathustra.

Nietzsche's appeal to power as the principle of all principles and the linking of this to any future theology requires some reorientation in

---

18. "How can anyone today still submit to the simplicity of Christian theologians to the point of insisting with them that the development of the conception of God from the 'God of Israel,' the god of a people, to the Christian God, the quintessence of everything good, represents *progress*? Yet even Renan does this. As if Renan had the right to be simpleminded! After all, the opposite stares you in the face. When the presuppositions of *ascending* life, when everything strong, brave, masterful, and proud is eliminated from the conception of God; when he degenerates step by step into a mere symbol, a staff for the weary, a sheet anchor for the drowning; when he becomes the god of the poor, the sinners, and the sick par excellence, and the attribute 'Savior' or 'Redeemer' remains in the end as the one essential attribute of divinity—just *what* does such a transformation signify? what, such a *reduction* of the divine?," *The Antichrist*, 584.

19. *Thus Spake Zarathrustra*, 226, 227. See also Friedrich Nietzsche, *The Will to Power*, trans Walter Kaufmann and R. J. Hollingdale (New York: Random House, 1967), particularly book 3, pt. 2: "The Will to Power in Nature," 332–81. It is here that Nietzsche searches for a viable concept of God, one that would depict him not as a causal agency but rather as "a maximal state, as an epoch—a point in the evolution of the will to power," 340.

our thinking and speaking about God. It also requires some reorientation in our thinking about justice and about the role of ethics and morality more generally. Given that this newfound principle of all principles is "beyond good and evil," the bearing it has on the requirement for justice in civil society becomes particularly problematic. Plainly enough, the will to power as the dynamics of master morality enables one to live *above* the stultifying norms of slave morality. But what remains troublesome is the lack of any specification of constraints of power that would inhibit living *below* the demands of justice within the social fabric.

There is no doubt that power plays a dominant role in Nietzsche's transvalued morality. It is power that supplies the condition for the trans-valuation of all hitherto existing values. In this role it is predominately re-active. It reacts against the stultifying values of slave morality and against the moral deity of Christianity in the role of the "highest value." Power enables one to be liberated from the shackles of a good and bad conscience that is condemned to follow the dictates of the herd and its repressive norms.

But in what sense is power also *proactive*? Power provides the conditions of freedom *from*, but does it also provide the conditions of freedom *to* and *for*? Clearly, it will not do to "recall" or "retrieve" previously existing values, for these are all irremediably tainted. To be sure, there is an "eternal return" that travels with Nietzsche's transvaluation of value, but this is neither a return informed by the Platonic doctrine of recollection nor by Heideggerian notions of repetition and commemoration. Master morality is not an exercise of revisiting old values and reclothing them in new garments. It is considerably more revolutionary. Old altars have to be destroyed before new ones can be built. "The raising of an altar requires the breaking of an altar," writes Nietzsche in his *Genealogy of Morals*.[20] The doctrine of the eternal return does not teach a retrieval of traditional values; rather it teaches an eternal return of the opportune and privileged moment in which new values are created. In this context, one must not forget the inscription on the gateway to the eternal return: *The Moment.*

The will to power, in its proactive expression, becomes a call to creativity. But in this call to creativity the call of moral conscience has been muted. The call of the will to power is a call to a region beyond good and evil. The good cannot create, we are told by Zarathustra: "For the good are *unable* to create; they are always the beginning of the end;

---

20. Friedrich Nietzsche, *The Birth of Tragedy and Genealogy of Morals,* trans. Francis Golff-ing (Garden City, N.Y.: Doubleday, 1956), 228.

they crucify him who writes new values on new tablets; they sacrifice the future to *themselves*—they crucify all man's future."[21] What is required is a creation of self that is informed by aesthetic possibilities rather than ethical imperatives. It is thus the moment of transvaluation in Nietzsche's heralded transvaluation of value takes on an aesthetic orientation and we finally learn that we have art so as not to die of truth and that it is only in the aesthetic phenomenon that life finds its justification.[22] Given such a predominant emphasis on the aesthetic, we can understand why any alliance of the will to power with the requirement for justice in civil society is destined to be met with considerable obstacles.

There is also a problem with Nietzsche's reticence about the connection of power and love in the consummate scheme of things. Clearly, the love that informs our personal and social existence is not powerless. The efficacy of love is not without power. Yet, Nietzsche's intensified fear that love degenerates into pity, succumbing to slave morality, precludes any positive teaching on love in Zarathustra's message. Love all too easily becomes an instrument of the "pitiful," the weak who have botched and bungled their existence and who use their condition to elicit pity from the strong so as to enslave them into the bonds of commiseration. Thus, even among those who want to be pitied, we can observe the traces of a will to power, a will to reduce one who has achieved self-mastery to a condition of servitude. Nietzsche is of the mind that even in the throes of love, one finds disguised power relations. Construed against the backdrop of what would appear to be a Hegelian-like structure of consciousness, with its master and servant struggle to the bitter end, power continues to hold the trump card. "Whoever knows the human heart guesses how poor, helpless, pretentious, and blundering even the best and deepest love is—it destroys more easily than it saves!"[23]

Readers of the texts of Nietzsche and Kierkegaard will find it odd that these two authors could join forces in their respective works *The Antichrist* and *Attack upon "Christendom"* and then part company in the writing of *The Will to Power* and *Works of Love*. Unlike Kierkegaard, Nietzsche was unable to move beyond the strictures of a virtue-ethic in dealing with the phenomenon of gift giving. This in great measure accounted for his truncated notion of love, in which love is little more than a negative expression of the will to power. Gift giving, the lynchpin

21. *Thus Spake Zarathrustra*, 324–25.

22. Friedrich Nietzsche, *The Birth of Tragedy and the Case of Wagner,* trans. with commentary by Walter Kaufmann (New York: Vintage Books, 1967), 52.

23. Friedrich Neitzsche, *Beyond Good and Evil,* trans. Marianne Cowan (Chicago: Gateway Editions, 1955), 222.

of a loving relationship, remains for Nietzsche a virtue, a moral property defining the moral self. The gift of love remains within the economy of a virtue-based ethic. Surely Nietzsche of all thinkers should have seen, as Kierkegaard clearly did, that the gift is genuinely beyond good and evil as a network of moral predicates. The gift is not itself a virtue. It is beyond and otherwise than virtue, transforming and transfiguring the discourses and actions within the production and exchange relations that govern the moral economy.

Nietzsche provides us with a quite clear illustration of reactive atheism. Freud provides us with another illustration. However, in spite of some superficial similarities, reactive atheism assumes a different posture in the two iconoclasts, and each has its own story to tell in the theism versus atheism controversy. The difference between Nietzsche and Freud has to do both with the state of affairs against which their reactions are framed and the envisioned telos that motivates the reaction in each. Freud's reactive atheism follows the route of psychological and anthropological critique. As also in the case of Nietzsche, the classical theistic concept of God also falls under indictment. This occurs, however, not because of its philosophical and theological misdirections but because of implications within Freud's metapsychology and his psychoanalytical practice.

Freud's reactive atheism is first of all a psychological atheism, elaborated against the backdrop of a general psychoanalytical theory of the psyche that demarcates the conscious from the unconscious and locates the economy of the psyche within the oft tumultuous commerce between the ego, the superego, and the id. This general metascientific theory of the psyche supplies the psychological protocols for Freud's demonstration that the concept of God can be analyzed into an extension of the father-figure image. Given Freud's view of nature as basically unfriendly to human purposes, pitiless and inexorable, red in tooth and claw, the human psyche responds to nature's onslaughts by creating a heavenly father patterned after an earthly father who was ever ready to provide protection and solace during one's infantile helplessness: "When the child grows up and finds that he is destined to remain a child for ever, and that he can never do without protection against unknown and mighty powers, he invests these with the traits of the father-figure; he creates for himself the gods, of whom he is afraid, whom he seeks to propitiate, and to whom he nevertheless entrusts the task of protecting him. Thus the longing-for-the-father explanation is identical with the other, the need for protection against the consequences of human weakness."[24]

24. Sigmund Freud, *The Future of an Illusion*, trans. W. D. Robson-Scott (New York: H. Liveright, 1953), 42.

In a state of helplessness, feeling weak and insecure, the adult, destined to remain forever a child, wishes for a divine protectorate and straightway "creates" one. Reminiscent of Ludwig Feuerbach on this point, who inverted the truth of the biblical account in Genesis to announce that it is man who creates God in his own image, Freud is able to fashion an explanation of the concept of God, construed as a heavenly father, as the end product in a hermeneutic of wish fulfillment. Religion, in its most general expression, is a system of wish illusions incompatible with reality.

This is the first stage of Freud's scientific explanation of religion. There is, however, another stage in the explanation. Not only is religion a web of wish illusions called upon to help us through difficult times, it is also a universal obsessive neurosis. If the belief in a heavenly father were merely an illusory projection, then it would be as innocuous as a belief in the existence of Santa Claus. But it is not simply that. It is also an illness, a form of neurosis, something from which one is to be delivered rather than a source of inspiration. This supplementary explanation is the result of Freud's grafting his psychological explanation of the concept of God as an extension of the father image onto a psychoanalytical theory of obsessive neurosis, and it is this move to the psychopathological that is designed by Freud to supply the coffin nails for any vestige of validity concerning matters of religious belief and practice. Not only is religion a cop-out in facing the slings and arrows of a recalcitrant nature and an oppressive civilization, it is in the end an illness, a universal obsessive neurosis, a malady that requires a cure rather than a theological account.

Freud's explanation of religion as obsessive neurosis has its roots, as do all forms of neurosis for Freud, in the Oedipus complex. The Oedipus complex, which arises from the instinctual attraction of the male child to the mother, coupled with an instinctual hatred of and rebellion against the father, is interpreted as playing a role, indeed a quite decisive one, in the relation of the believer to his illusory heavenly father. The story of the relation of the believer to his projected heavenly father follows the scenario of the individual neurosis in the life of the male child, which unfolds as a rebellion followed by guilt, guilt followed by remorse and repentance, and remorse and repentance followed by the desire for restoration through unconditional obedience. Caught up in the triangulation of libidinal drives, overemotionalized attachment to the mother, and rebellion against the father, the male child is destined to suffer the pangs of guilt and seek to be restored into good graces with his father. So too we mortals as "sons" of the heavenly father are disposed to appeal to doctrines of sin and salvation and a rigorous morality so as to overcome our alienation with our created deity.

This psychoanalytical explanation of religion as a system of wish illusions and a universal obsessive neurosis is then aligned with an anthropological critique of religious beliefs and practices. The individual neurosis of humankind finds its analog in the history of the human race. In his anthropological studies, Freud investigated the origins of the murder and incest taboos, tracing them back to the killing of the primordial father in early patriarchal society. The chieftain of the tribal unit, so runs Freud's account, kept all of the females as his wives and expelled the sons from the tribe, setting the stage for a rebellion on the part of the sons. Suffering remorse for having killed the tribal patriarch and violating the boundaries of blood relations by intermarrying with the wives collected by their father, the sons pledged fidelity to the two universal taboos of murder and incest to avoid any recurrence of the unseemly deeds in which they took part. It was thus the two commandments "Thou shalt not commit murder" and "Thou shalt not commit incest" became inscribed in our individual and social history.

To what extent Freud's speculative hermeneutic of the ways of the psyche and the history of the human race is able to engender support and agreement on the part of psychologists and anthropologists is an issue to which responses remain mixed. The story Freud has to tell about "civilization and its discontents" appears to be very much a grand narrative, and consequently it has provoked stout critical reactions from certain philosophers and psychologists who have reservations about grand narratives. Lacanian psychoanalysis is clearly a case in point. Importing the linguistic turn into psychoanalysis, Jacques Lacan attacked both the theory of libidinal energy and the framework of mechanical causation in classical Freudian psychoanalysis. Utilizing the resources of linguistics he then proceeded to reinterpret the unconscious as a forgotten language rather than as a reservoir of biologically determined instinctual urges.[25]

A more direct broadside against the Freudian metapsychology and therapeutic strategy was discharged by philosopher Gilles Deleuze and his psychiatrically trained collaborator, Félix Guattari. In developing their program of schizo-analysis, designed to replace the psychoanalysis of Freud, Deleuze and Guattari never tire of harpooning Freud's metapsychology, which they see as a monument to arborescent constructivism. The principle of all principles in Freud's theory construction is the "reduction to the One," whereby everything is traced back to "the single Father," explaining all the varied dimensions of human behavior by way

25. See particularly Jacques Lacan, *The Language of the Self: The Function of Language in Psychoanalysis,* trans. Anthony Wilden (Baltimore, Md.: Johns Hopkins University Press, 1968).

of the Oedipus complex.[26] Somewhat more sympathetic to Freud's program, reinterpreting Freud's concept of the unconscious against the backdrop of the dynamics of a semiotic/symbolic interaction, Julia Kristeva has maneuvered a path between an uncritical appropriation and an outright rejection of Freud's historic accomplishments in the field of psychiatry.[27]

Our task in the current project is not that of assessing the contributions and limitations of Freud's metapsychology and cultural anthropology. It is rather that of learning something from his reactive atheism. However limited, or even misdirected, his scientific explanation of religion may be, he has in his own serendipitous manner pointed to a major problem in the classical concept of God, namely that of a tendency toward anthropomorphism. Traveling with the linking of God with the concept of being in traditional metaphysics, whereby God becomes construed as a supernatural being, we find a predilection to appeal to highly personalized attributes in defining his nature. Not only is God characterized as being wise, good, merciful, just, and forgiving, he also has certain social roles assigned to him—lord, sovereign, judge, and of course father. Admittedly, these are attributes understood to apply to God in a manner quite different from the way they describe human qualities, traits of character, and social roles. God is a "person" in some superlative sense. Yet, the fact remains that he is conceptualized as a person, as a Thou who remains within the economy of the I-Thou encounter. God as a person, even if in the superlative sense of personhood, remains a being among other beings, subject to the ontological and ontic determinations drawn from an analysis of finite beings in general. God conceived in this manner quickly becomes a subject for the assignation of anthropomorphic properties.

That such a concept of the Deity is unable to sustain our religious interests and our philosophical sensibilities becomes particularly evident when classical theism butts up against the intractable problem of evil. Impaled on the horns of a dilemma, requiring that God as a supernatural being is both omnipotent and omnibenevolent, evil results either from God's lack of power to overcome it or from his lack of goodness that keeps him from doing that which he apparently is able to do. It is precisely the attribution of personality traits of will, freedom, and moral qualities that places the Deity in this predicament. He either lacks the freedom and the

26. Gilles Deleuze and Félix Guattari, *A Thousand Plateaus: Capitalism and Schizophrenia*, trans. Brian Massumi (Minneapolis: University of Minnesota Press, 1987), 31.

27. See particularly Julia Kristeva, *Revolution in Poetic Language*, trans. Margaret Waller (New York: Columbia University Press, 1984).

will to overcome evil or he lacks the requisite moral traits to do so. As long as God is considered to be a Thou, a person endowed with freedom, will, and moral designs, the problem of evil will remain a conundrum from both the side of divinity and the side of humanity, leading eventually to a portrayal of the Deity as either an invincible tyrant or a powerless sovereign.

It was the genius of Spinoza to detect this anthropomorphic flaw in traditional theism. Although Spinoza remained within the tradition of onto-theology, insisting on the definition of God as "Infinite Substance," he was able to maneuver an internal critique of the classical portrait of the Deity by straightway rejecting the applicability of will and design to the being of God. To be sure, he was able to speak of God as "free cause." By this, however, he meant that God "acts from the laws of His own nature only, and is compelled by no one. . . . Hence, it follows there is no cause, either external to God or within Him, which can incite Him to act except the perfection of His own nature."[28] There can be neither an internal nor an external cause of God's action. If he were impelled to act by virtue of an internal cause, this would mean that God desires something he now lacks, and hence he would be imperfect. Nor can he be impelled by an external ideal or telos, which would constrain him. He acts from the necessity of his own nature; and only in this sense can he be properly spoken of as being free.

What one finds in Spinoza's internal critique of classical theism is a highlighting of the pitfalls of anthropomorphism in its various guises. Free will and design are not properties that can appropriately be ascribed to God. If theism proceeds from the framework of a person-to-person encounter, a finite self encountering an infinite self, an immanental thou addressing a putative transcendent thou, the stage for a justified reactive atheism, like that of Freud, is set in motion. God is destined to become an elevated father figure, a superlative supreme court judge, a sovereign of all that he surveys, a legislator greater than which none can be conceived. It may well be that a lasting contribution of Freud's reactive atheism is to have shown the misdirections in a theism that proceeds from person-ascribing properties.

At this juncture, the reactive atheism of Nietzsche and Freud would appear to be in substantial agreement. In both cases there is a reaction against the concept of God as a supernatural being endowed with idealized personal traits. But the two versions of atheism soon part company.

28. Spinoza, "Ethics," Prop. 42, in *Spinoza Selections*, ed. John Wild, The Modern Students Library (New York: Charles Scribner's Sons, 1930), 114.

Whereas Nietzsche's dismissal of the theo-metaphysics of a Platonized Christianity amounts to a strategy of deconstruction that opens an inquiry into a new sense of divinity yet to be named, Freud forecloses any such inquiry, unable to find any interesting sense of the divine on the other side of his reactive atheism. There is no alternative concept of God that might stand in for that of classical theism, except possibly the lowercase "god *logos*" that Freud hurriedly analyzes into "science." And this science, we are instructed, unlike religion, is not an illusion: "No, science is no illusion. But it would be an illusion to suppose that we could get anywhere else what it cannot give us."[29]

Another atheistic perspective on the reaction against classical theism is put forward by Jean-Paul Sartre. Whereas Nietzsche's atheism might be dubbed postmodernist, and Freud's psychological, Sartre's version could be named existentialist. Sartre sketches his atheistic project against the backdrop of what he came to call "existential psychoanalysis" as an alternative to Freud's "empirical psychoanalysis." In this sketch he rejects some of the principal presuppositions of Freud's metapsychology and radically revises some of the others. He jettisons Freud's primacy of the Oedipus complex and substitutes for it the primacy of choice. He undermines Freud's postulation of the unconscious by arguing that the datum at issue, namely repression, can be better explained by the effects of bad faith and the reflexivity of the "I" and the "Me" within the structure of consciousness. Existential freedom replaces Freud's mechanistically modeled determinism. And the desire for pleasure, the libidinal basis of Freudian psychoanalysis, gives way to the desire to be God. Sartre, however, does agree with Freud that an understanding of the structure and dynamics of human existence requires that one proceed beyond the secondary and superficial manifestations of personal behavior so as to arrive at the fundamental project that underlies all human striving and comprises its ultimate goal. But this fundamental project, unlike that defined by Freud, is not the will-to-pleasure but rather the will and desire to be God—a will and a desire that for Sartre are destined to remain unfulfilled.[30]

29. Freud, *The Future of an Illusion*, 94, 98, cf. pp. 86–87: "Man cannot remain a child for ever; he must venture at last into the hostile world. This may be called 'education to reality'; . . . And man is not entirely without means of assistance; since the time of the deluge science has taught him much, and it will still further increase his power. . . . Then with one of our comrades in unbelief he will be able to say without regret: Let us leave the heavens to the angels and the sparrows."

30. Jean-Paul Sartre, *Being and Nothingness: An Essay on Phenomenological Ontology*, trans Hazel E. Barnes (New York: Philosophical Library, 1956), 557–75.

Freud and Sartre are both atheists, but their respective positions afford different lessons. Freud's atheism is a psychological atheism based on allegedly scientific investigations of the structure and dynamics of the human psyche. Sartre's atheism is rooted in certain existential and phenomenological ruminations on the problem of being. His reactive atheism needs to be understood against the backdrop of the central focus of his major work, *Being and Nothingness*. In this work the problem of being unfolds as a story about a rupture of two quite distinct modalities or spheres. There is being in the mode of the "in-itself" (*en-soi*) and there is being in the mode of the "for-itself" (*pour-soi*). The former is being as a plenitude—fixed, full, complete, without potency, devoid of any becoming. The latter is being as vacuous, fluid, incomplete, perpetually in process of becoming that which it is not yet. One quickly recognizes that being-in-itself is for Sartre the mode of being that defines the inert world of objects and things, whereas being-for-itself designates the being we ourselves are, highlighting the existential features of freedom, choice, and responsibility. These two modes of being are understood as incompatible, and it is thus that any effort on the part of being-for-itself to constitute itself as being-in-itself must end in failure.

But it is precisely such a unification of the two modes of being that defines the classical concept of God as a being who contains the fullness of reality within himself. Human reality, in its desire to be God, attempts to achieve this fullness; but in doing so it stands the risk of losing itself: "Each human reality is at the same time a direct project to metamorphose its own For-itself into an In-itself-For-itself and a project of the appropriation of the world as a totality of being-in-itself, in the form of a fundamental quality. Every human reality is a passion in that it projects losing itself so as to found being and by the same stroke to constitute the In-itself which escapes contingency by being its own foundation, the *Ens causa sui*, which religions call God. Thus the passion of man is the reverse of that of Christ, for man loses himself as man in order that God may be born. But the idea of God is contradictory and we lose ourselves in vain. Man is a useless passion."[31]

The fundamental project of human existence, which replaces the foundational desire for pleasure within the Freudian scheme of things, is to attain the impermeability, solidity, density, and fullness of being-in-itself. This would enable the self to fill the vacuity, the "nothingness," that pervades its existence. The realization of such a project would provide an antidote to the anxiety of nonbeing—the anxiety over unactu-

31. Ibid., 615.

alized potentialities in one's past and the anxiety over future choices yet to be made. Using its passion and freedom the for-itself strives for a unification—indeed coincidence—of being-in-itself and being-for-itself, thus overcoming the perplexing contingencies of life by securing its own foundation. Such a life would be without anxiety, without despair, without the dread of becoming that thrusts one into an unknown future. But such an idea and ideal is self-contradictory, for in the moment the self would become a synthetic unity of for-itself and in-itself, it would lose itself as for-itself. Now such an unbroken solidarity of being-in-itself and being-for-itself is precisely that which characterizes the being of the God of classical theism, in which God is defined as an infinite and supremely perfect being. Hence, the very idea of God is self-contradictory, and the fundamental desire to give birth to God is destined to suffer a profound metaphysical frustration.

Sartre's reactive atheism takes the form of a peculiar inversion of the classical ontological argument for the existence of God. God, defined as that being than which nothing greater can be conceived (Anselm) or as the supremely perfect being (Descartes), *necessarily cannot exist* because the existence of such a being would be internally self-contradictory. What is of some note here is that Sartre's atheism, unlike that of Freud, exhibits an ontological rather than a psychological trajectory, and hence it figures as a more direct response to the linking of the question about God to the problem of being in the history of theo-metaphysics.

What is not pursued by Sartre, however, is an interrogation of the consequences of a possible *de*coupling of the question of God from the problem of being. Might it be that the very notion of an *ens causa sui,* whether articulated in the grammar of classical theism as a supremely existing perfect being or in the grammar of Sartre as the perfect coin-cidence of being-in-itself and being-for-itself, is in the end a misplaced referent in speaking about the Deity? Might it be that the controversy between Sartre and his theistic opponents, and the longstanding dispute between atheists and theists more generally, ultimately dissolves into a quixotic scenario of either affirming or denying theocentric windmills? Let us suppose that the object of interrogation, that which is to be proved or disproved, the putative conclusion of the finely tuned arguments by theists and atheists alike, falls victim to a species of the fallacy of mis-placed concreteness. The concept of God as the synthetic totality of the modes of being-in-itself and being-for-itself may well, as Sartre argues, land us in a contradiction. But instead of this providing the concluding sentence in an essay on phenomenological ontology, it perhaps should rather be the opening sentence in an investigation of a possible space that is otherwise than being.

Alterity and Transcendence

The discussions in the preceding sections have nudged us to inquire about a possible space at the extremities of the being-problem as it relates to the question about God. Our investigations of the marriage of metaphysics and theology in classical theism; the epistemological and linguistic turns in modernity; the entwinement of language, being, and God; the concept of God in postmodernity; and the contributions of reactive atheism have all pointed in the direction of a terrain of signification on the hither side of not only the categories of metaphysics but also the probings of fundamental ontology. It is thus that one must undertake the quite formidable task of elucidating what is at issue in speaking about what resides "beyond" the range of metaphysics and ontology and which consequently can be spoken of as otherwise than being.

Insofar as the grammar of otherwise than being has been used from time to time in the writings of Levinas, Derrida, and Marion, intermittent engagements with their contributions on the topic will become unavoidable. All three recognize clearly enough that the locutions of "beyond" and "otherwise than" find one of their most explicit sources in book VI of Plato's *Republic,* where Socrates introduces the simile of the divided line to explain the correlative distinctions between knowledge and opinion and being and becoming. After having established that opinion (*doxa*) remains mired in a changing world of becoming and that only knowledge (*epistēmē*) can lay hold of the world of rigorous being, Socrates instructs Glaucon that there is still to be considered the Good, which as the author of knowledge and all things known exceeds even being in power and dignity. The Good, in short, is *epekeina tes ousias.*

Without examining the multiple nuances in the meaning of the terms here conjoined, *epekeina* and *ousias,* and the multiple interpretations of these nuances that have become extant, there are some straightforward observations that help to clear the path for further inquiry. The play of "beyond," "above," "otherwise than," "surpassing," and "transcendent to," in various configurations of cross reference, appear to inform the meaning of *epekeina. Ousia,* as is well known, also invites multiple semantic nuances—being in the sense of the *isness* of *to be,* in the sense of the totality of beings, in the sense of essence as an intrinsic defining feature, in the sense of substance understood as what underlies and in some sense supports attributes and properties, in the sense of existentiality, and no doubt in other senses as well. On this point Aristotle would seem to have gotten it right: *being* is said in many ways!

In the multiple senses of *epekeina,* it is important to note that the discontinuity at issue—otherwise than, above, beyond—is not the discon-

tinuity of a pure negativity as an explicit denial. It is rather the discontinuity of a robust transcendence that places the Good outside the reach
of the categories of being. Glaucon's response to this characterization of
the Good by Socrates is not unexpected: What a magnificent hyperbole;
by the light of heaven how amazing! And hyperbolic, one needs add, in
the sense of exceeding and surpassing.

The story of the *epekeina tes ousias* does not, however, end with
the philosophy of Plato. The thematic of otherwise than being was continued by Plotinus in his doctrine of the One as elevated beyond the
range of Nous, or Mind, and was then revisited in the Neoplatonism of
the fourth and fifth centuries, particularly in the negative theology of
Pseudo-Dionysius. Although Plato was careful not to conflate the Good
with the idea of God, in Plotinian mysticism and in the Neoplatonism of
the church fathers the distinction became blurred, leading to an amalgam of the Good and God as otherwise than being. Pseudo-Dionysius,
however, was insistent that this denial of God as a being was not to be
understood as a contentless negative determination. To be sure, the *via
negativa* compels us to say that God "is not." But the negative at issue here
itself undergoes a negation in that what is attested to is not the absence
of reality but rather a *superabundance* of reality. Hence, Pseudo-Dionysius
is able to speak about the Deity as *huperousios*—as superessentiality and
superexistentiality. To say that God is not is to say that he is *more* than can
be articulated about him through categories of being that one would
ordinarily recognize.

To expand our clarification of the vocabulary of otherwise than
being as a radical transcendence, it is indeed helpful to trace its impact
upon later modes of thought. But also it is important to return time and
again to Plato's dialogues, specifically to the disquisition on the concept
of being in the *Sophist* and the nonconcept of the *khora* in the *Timaeus*.

It is in the *Sophist* that Plato subjects the being-problem to a rigorous
and intensive examination. The discussion turns on what Plato names the
"greatest kinds" or "superforms"—being, sameness, difference, motion,
and rest. What is disclosed is that some of these greatest kinds combine
or blend while others do not. Being, sameness, and difference all happily
combine with each other, while motion and rest combine with being,
sameness, and difference, but motion cannot combine with rest and rest
cannot combine with motion. The lesson to be learned from this is that
our search for knowledge needs be governed by an understanding of that
which combines and that which does not. Principles of inclusion and
exclusion, conjunction and disjunction, ontologically secured, provide
the foundation for knowledge. Quadruped combines with horse, but
a person would be mistaken to believe that quadruped combines with

ostrich. Knowledge is made possible by the natural cleavages within the structure of being, a structure that falls out as a manifold landscape of forms of artifacts, forms of natural kinds, mathematical forms, moral forms, and the forms of the greatest kinds. Veritably, in Plato's kingdom of forms, there are many mansions!

Against this backdrop of entwined ontological and epistemological commitments, Plato's position on the role of negativity in negative statements can be understood. Only by getting clear on the play of negativity will one be in position to counter the claim of Parmenides that "what is" cannot in any sense "not be," and that which "is not" cannot in any sense "be." In recognizing that motion and rest do not combine, cannot be conjoined, one can truthfully say that motion "is not" rest. But this does not entail a denial of the reality of motion. It is rather to say that motion is *different from* rest. Negation thus boils down not to a claim for absence but to a recognition of difference. Both motion and rest retain their residence in the citadel of being. They blend with being by virtue of the fact they are; they blend with sameness in that they both exhibit a self-identity, they remain identical with themselves; and they blend with difference in that each resists combination with the other.

The lesson to be learned from this dialectical play within the space of the superforms is that negation, in the guise of nonbeing, should be understood specifically with the help of the superform of difference. As such, nonbeing needs to be accorded a place in the world of forms. Nonbeing retains an unbroken liaison with being. Indeed, it plays a role in the very *constitution* of being in that every instance of being appears within a horizon of finite determinations of what it is and infinite determinations of what it is not. It is only through a recognition of the relational character of nonbeing, nonbeing as *relative* rather than *absolute,* that positive and negative statements can be explained in a meaningful way.

In the genealogy of the use and understanding of nonbeing from Parmenides to Plato to Plotinus to Pseudo-Dionysius to Hegel and beyond, it is important not to gloss the contribution by Plato in his *Sophist.* Nonbeing can be analyzed into the otherness of difference, and difference, plainly enough, remains within the structure of being. How this construal of negation and nonbeing in terms of otherness and difference in the *Sophist* impacts on the *epekeina tes ousias* of the Good in the *Republic* remains one of those particularly knotty hermeneutical questions. The Good does not appear to play a major role in the *Sophist.* If it were to play a major role, would it still be otherwise than being, transcending even the forms of the greatest kinds, including sameness as identity and otherness as difference? Suppose that the Good were to maintain its lofty perch beyond the structures of being, then one would need to install another sense of otherness so as to distinguish the transcendence of the Good from otherness as difference within the determinations of being.

As the *Sophist* provides Plato's most explicit statement on the problem of being as it relates to nonbeing as otherness, so the *Timaeus* presents a narrative about that which resides on the fringe of any discourse on being. The narrative congeals into a "likely story" in which the *khora,* commonly translated as "the receptacle," becomes the central theme. Discourse about the *khora* is more myth than logos, illustrating at best a species of "bastard reasoning" because the subject matter of the discourse escapes the forms of being as proper objects of knowledge.[32] The *khora* is not a form, and in no wise is it a being or a collection of beings; but neither is it pure nothingness or brute nonbeing. Yet, it enters our discourse as a factor in the explanation of the cosmos. The Good and the eternal and immutable forms alone are unable to account for the empirical world of becoming.

One needs to speak of the *khora* in mythopoetic terms. It is the "nurse of becoming"; it is the "mother" that furnishes the place for the seeds of generation and growth; it is a "room" where things come to be and pass away. Yet, it is not a void where things are not. It is formless, but it has a capacity to receive form, which suggests that it is like a receptacle. It is something akin to a space *in which* things appear. As such, it exhibits some similarity to Aristotle's notion of prime matter. But it is not strictly convertible with the Aristotelian notion. Prime matter designates that *out of which* things are made; the receptacle designates that *in which* things appear. Yet it is not a nameless void, nor is it the dimensional space of two, three, four, or more dimensions. The texture of the space that is the receptacle would thus appear to elude all of our trustworthy categorial signifiers. Derrida, on this point, helps us to move about in the semantic thicket when he writes: "If the *khora* receives everything, it does not do this in the manner of a medium or of a container, not even that of a receptacle, because the receptacle is yet a figure inscribed in it. This is neither an intelligible extension, in the Cartesian sense, a receptive

32. Julia Kristeva calls our attention to the difficulty of speaking about the *khora* in forms of intelligibility that one might recognize when she cites as the principal function of the term "to denote an essentially mobile and extremely provisional articulation constituted by movements and their ephemeral stases." She then continues, "Our discourse—all discourse—moves with and against the *chora* in the sense that it simultaneously depends upon and refuses it. Although the *chora* can be designated and regulated, it can never be definitely posited: as a result one can situate the *chora* and, if necessary, lend it a topology, but one can never give it axiomatic form," *Revolution in Poetic Language,* 25–26.

subject, in the Kantian sense of *intuitus derivativus,* nor a pure sensible space, as a form of receptivity."[33]

Closely allied with the *khora* as a formless receptacle is the quasi-phenomenon of "necessity," the "errant" or "wandering" cause that keeps the empirical world of becoming short of a perfect exemplification of the Good. Everything in the empirical world falls short of perfection. Necessity thus functions not only as a protoprinciple of indeterminacy but also as a factor of distortion and frustration for the *demiourgos,* the maker and father of all things, who has the onerous task of making his creation as good as it can possibly be. To do so, however, he has to "persuade" necessity, working against rather formidable odds in fashioning the cosmos in such a manner as not to be wholly alien to human striving.

It is at this juncture that Plato's "likely story" about the receptacle, the demiurge, and necessity, converge with the narratives of classical Christianity and Judaism, without, however, becoming coincident with them. The principal point at issue turns on whether necessity as the errant cause provides a sufficient explanation for evil. It would seem that Plato would be required to offer a negative response to the suggestion that necessity is somehow a proximate cause of evil. Evil for Plato is not stitched into the warp and woof of the cosmos. It arises from the misdirected thoughts and activities of rational souls. One might say that necessity functions as one of the conditions for the presence of evil, but the cause of evil will need to be sought elsewhere.

The problem of evil, and the acceleration of efforts to devise a theodicy whereby to justify the ways of God given the undeniable occurrence of evil in his creation, was quickly taken up by the church fathers and medieval theologians, both Christian and Jewish, many of whom were steeped in Greek philosophy. Particularly in the thought of Saint Augustine the Platonic heritage becomes discernible, especially on matters having to do with good and evil. If God is supremely good and his creation is deemed to be a finite good, and if indeed everything that is made by God is not only good but *very* good, whence evil? Is evil to be equated with absolute nonbeing or possibly with something like Plato's necessity as errant cause in the receptacle, which although it is not absolute nonbeing clearly borders on it? Both Plato and Augustine stopped short of equating evil with nonbeing. Yet, Augustine is quite clear on the matter of nonbeing playing a role in the origin of evil: "Although the will derives its existence, as a nature, from its creation by God, its falling away from its true being is due to its creation out of nothing. Yet

33. Derrida, "How to Avoid Speaking: Denials," 106.

man did not fall away to the extent of losing all being; but when he turned toward himself his being was less real than when he adhered to him who exists in the supreme degree. And so, to abandon God and to exist in oneself, that is to please oneself, is not immediately to lose all being; but it is to come nearer to nothingness."[34]

The problem of the relation of evil to nonbeing thus becomes a peculiarly troublesome one in both the Platonic and the Augustinian-Christian traditions. Plato's *khora,* which houses the errant cause that provides a condition for evil, is clearly otherwise than being. But it is also clear that the *khora* is not otherwise than being in the same sense that the Good is *epekeina tes ousias.* Although the Good is otherwise than being, not all that which is otherwise than being is good. The Good is truly "beyond" or "above" being, while the *khora* and the unpredictable things that it somehow contains are "below" being. They are both outside the chain or scale of being proceeding from the lowest to the highest, but the proper positioning of the two requires that the one be exalted while the other be debased.

With the conjugation of the Good with God in classical theism, particularly in the theism informed by the mysticism of Neoplatonism, certain complexities entered the forms of theological discourse. Classical theism was not prepared to sever the concept of God from the structures of being and continued to view God as the highest being, the being that crowns the scale of being and is in some manner the cause of the lower orders of being. However, in the Neoplatonism of the tradition of negative theology, a path was opened to a concept of the Deity quite beyond the structures of being, conjoined with Plato's Good as *huperousios,* beyond positive predication, beyond all negation—indeed beyond being itself.

Yet, a persisting ambiguity pervades the negative theologian's discourse about a *huperousios*—a superessentiality and superexistentiality—on the hither side of all positive predications. The negative predications of the *via negativa* are still "about" the Deity in some sense of being about. They are not indicators of an absence. They are allusions to a presence—admittedly a presence that can no longer be described by way of positive attributes, but a presence nonetheless. The God of negative theology is indeed "beyond" being in that he is not a being among other beings. He is *more* than a being specifiable within a categorial scheme. He *surpasses* the being of even the being that crowns the scale or great chain of being, but he is not devoid of being as presence. His being as presence is in *excess* of

34. Saint Augustine, *The City of God,* trans. Henry Scowcroft Bettensen (New York: Penguin Books, 1972), 572.

the being that is more commonly ascribed to beings within the economy of beings from the lowest to the highest. If we continue to scratch the underbelly of the *huperousios* of negative theology we are likely to find an exalted presence that permits its presence to be known only via negative predications. It is thus that even negative theology is unable to escape the constraints of a metaphysics of theism.

Such also would appear to be the case in Jean-Luc Marion's postmodern theology of "God without Being," in which there is a rather startling equivocation on the preposition *without*. Responding to a variety of critics of the first publication of his book *God without Being*, Marion makes an effort in his Preface to the English edition to set the record straight on what is at issue in the title of the book: "The whole book suffered from the inevitable and assumed equivocation of its title: was it insinuating that the God 'without being' is not, or does not exist? Let me repeat now the answer I gave then: no, definitely not. God is, exists, and that is the least of things. At issue here is not the possibility of God's attaining Being, but quite the opposite, the possibility of Being's attaining to God."[35] In the end, Marion's project looks very much like that of Pseudo-Dionysius. Marion's God without Being has the same identifying features as does the *huperousios* of negative theology. In both cases the Deity is identified as exceeding or surpassing Being, but not as displacing Being. And in attempting to clarify his position on this matter, Marion introduces another ambiguity, if not equivocation, when he writes "God is, exists, and that is the least of things." One surely cannot take *is* and *exists* as strictly convertible. Thus it appears we continue to be mired in an aporetics of classical metaphysical theism.

A more robust and radical notion of alterity and transcendence is thus required if one is to proceed beyond the inherent limitations in classical theism, a more radical probing of the very grammar about God, about the divine, about the holy. Such would seem to be precisely the path furrowed by Emmanuel Levinas in his reconfigured grammar of alterity and transcendence. God as otherwise than being, beyond the economy of sameness and otherness as outlined in the *Sophist*, cannot be named the "first Other," or the "other par excellence," or even as the "absolutely other." What is required is an even more accentuated hyperbole, the "other than the other" (*autre qu' autrui*), or "an alterity

---

35. Jean-Luc Marion, *God without Being: Hors-texte*, trans. Thomas A. Carlson (Chicago: University of Chicago Press, 1991), xix–xx.

prior to the alterity of the other," opening a vision of the "transcendent to the point of absence."[36]

The lesson to be learned from Levinas's accentuated hyperbole of God as other than the other is the requirement to sort out nuances in the meaning of otherness. Specifically, the sense of otherness used to articulate differences within the economy of being and its dyad of sameness (identity)/otherness (difference) needs to be distinguished from the sense of otherness as utterly transcendent to the economy of being. It is here that we arrive at a crucial juncture in our pursuit of the question about God as otherwise than being. Without this distinction between the two senses of otherness, the grammar of alterity and transcendence in speaking of the divinity and the holiness of God will remain clouded in impenetrable semantic mists.

Striving for maximal clarity on the issue at hand, it may be helpful to play with the distinction of "different from" versus "otherwise than." Alterity within the economy of being is that which is different from; alterity beyond the forms and categories of being is otherwise than. And coupled with these two senses of alterity or otherness are two senses of transcendence. In speaking of that which is transcendent, one is surely speaking of that which is in some sense other. But, again, one needs to monitor the polysemy that travels with the use of the concept of transcendence. Husserl found it necessary to speak of a "transcendence-within-immanence," a transcendence within the topography of transcendental subjectivity and its economy of the *ego-cogito-cogitata* intentionality complex. The *cogitata,* as the proper intentional objects of the *cogito,* transcend the acts of identification and constitution by the intend-

---

36. "God is not simply the 'first other', or the 'other *par excellence,*' or the 'absolutely other,' but other than the other, other otherwise, and other with an alterity prior to the alterity of the other, prior to the ethical obligation to the other and different from every neighbor, transcendent to the point of absence, to the point of his possible confusion with the agitation of the *there is,*" Emmanuel Levinas, *Of God Who Comes to Mind,* trans. Bettina Bergo (Stanford, Calif.: Stanford University Press, 1998), 69. Although Levinas does not stand in the tradition of Jewish mysticism, on the level of a first-order characterization of the Deity there are some remarkable similarities between Levinas's characterization of God not simply as the first other but the other than the other and Rabbi David A. Cooper's kabbalistic description of God in his provocative volume, *God Is a Verb: Kabbalah and the Practice of Mystical Judaism* (New York: Riverhead Books, 1997). Although Western mysticism for the most part has borrowed schema and categories from the metaphysical tradition, there are some exceptions and the esoteric teaching of kabbalah, at least as articulated by Rabbi Cooper, would appear to be such an exception. God as a *verb* rather than as a noun shifts attention away from construing the Deity as a being, even if conceived as a supernatural entity. God as a verb is indeed *huperousios,* and indeed in a quite robust sense.

ing consciousness. Consciousness is always *of* something. The object as intended, the "object-as-meant," indeed phenomenon in the strict understanding of the term, cannot be conflated with the intending act. Nor is the object-as-meant to be confused with the existing object. The celebrated phenomenological reduction requires that one suspend the existential status of the datum in question so as to lead one back (*reducere*) to the structure of meaning, elaborated in Husserl's intriguing but problematic doctrine of the "intuition of essences" (*Wesenschau*). One is able to observe in Husserl's elaborate program of phenomenological idealism varied senses of transcendence in play within the determinations of the structure of transcendental subjectivity—which becomes more elaborate as one moves to the region of transcendental intersubjectivity and eventually to the transcendental structure of the lifeworld (*Lebenswelt*).

Within the scope of Husserl's phenomenology, one is thus able to find variable senses of transcendence but all against the backdrop of a "transcendence-within-immanence," making use of what is designated here as the grammar of "different from" instead of "otherwise than." This is not yet a robust and radical sense of transcendence, and this is the case principally because Husserl's philosophical investigations were motivated by epistemological concerns in which transcendence took its coloring from the requirements of transcendental reflection. It is certainly not accidental that Husserl flagged his philosophical program as that of "transcendental phenomenological idealism." Granted, there is a deployment of a sense of transcendence in transcendental analysis, but this should never be confused with either metaphysical transcendence or the hyperbolic transcendence of an otherwise than being.

As the transcendence at issue in talk about that which is otherwise than being should be confused neither with the classical metaphysical perspective nor with its meaning in transcendental philosophy, so also it is of a different sort than that which is found in the existentialism of Jean-Paul Sartre. Sartre's existentialized notion of transcendence is wholly immanental. It is a descriptive designator used by Sartre to characterize the projective thrust of human existence. The being-for-itself that defines human reality for Sartre is a *pro-ject*. To be, characteristic of the for-itself, is to be projected into a future, opening the space for the surpassing of the present self as it moves into a future. The for-itself perpetually ceases to be what it is and becomes that which it is not yet. Herein resides the dynamics of transcendence, which is more a qualitative determination of an act than an encountered event or state of affairs. It is something that happens *in* time rather than *to* time. It is an occurrence within the economy of finitude and temporality. It is a quality of existence found in the depths of human action.

In our hunt for the more robust sense of transcendence, to which Levinas points us in his assorted hyperboles, one needs to begin with the contributions of classical metaphysics on the topic of transcendence. And in doing so, one needs to be attentive to a distinction that traveled with the history of the concept of being from the very beginning, namely the distinction between the "to be" of whatever is and "being" as pertaining to the different forms, levels, and kinds of being that make up the totality of things from great to small. It is this distinction, as we have already noted, that was given a decisive expression in the philosophy of Heidegger, requiring a sorting out of the types and terms of inquiry that distinguish fundamental ontology from metaphysics. Metaphysics, in Heidegger's scheme of things, falls out as an *ontic* analysis, geared to a delineation of the kinds of beings (*Seiendes*) and their formal determinations and causal connections. Fundamental ontology follows the route of an *ontological* analysis and sets its sights on an understanding of the meaning of "to be" (*Sein*), specifically of the "to be" as illustrated in the concerns and dealings of human existence (*Dasein*). Within the constraints of metaphysics, thus defined, the concept of God will have as its putative referent the highest possible kind of being. Such is precisely what happened in the history of classical theism with its designations of the Deity as an *ens realissimum* and an *ens causa sui*.

Plainly enough, there is in this classical theistic concept of God a notion of transcendence that proceeds beyond the transcendence-within-immanence of the epistemological paradigm of transcendental philosophy as well as beyond the constraints within Sartre's existential ontology. In the vocabulary of classical theism, God as a supernatural and infinitely perfect being is transcendent to the world of which he allegedly is the cause in a manner quite different from the way that the perceived object and the object-as-perceived transcend the act of perception. And clearly, classical theism would have no truck with Sartre's immanental notion of transcendence. Let us name the transcendence within the vocabulary of classical theism "metaphysical transcendence." The distinction between infinite being (*res infinita*) and finite being (*res finita*), theologically articulated as the distinction between *ens creator* and *ens creatum,* defines the terms that figure in the use and understanding of metaphysical transcendence. God as infinite cause and creator is transcendent to the finite world that comprises his creation. And by this we are to understand that God is self-sufficient and wholly independent, in every respect constitutive of the finite world, while the finite world is absolutely nonconstitutive of God. Within the economy of the totality of beings, God as being in the superlative sense, as that being than which none greater or more perfect can be conceived, crowns the scale of being that proceeds from the lowest to the highest.

Admittedly, variations on the status and quality of transcendence in classical theism have appeared from time to time. The pantheism of Spinoza, in which the distinction between *natura naturans* and *natura naturata* exhibits an internal rather than an external relation, is an example of such a variation, as is also the perspective of panentheism in the process theology of Charles Hartshorne. But these variations are still variations of classical theism, and they continue to make purchases on metaphysical modes of thought in an effort to find the proper referent for the concept of God.

Aside from the notorious difficulties in mounting compelling arguments for the existence of such a special sort of being—arguments that are revisited time and again in the works of speculative theology and philosophy of religion—there is the existentially oriented concern over whether such a being is able to sustain our concrete religious interests. It is this concern that is raised when Heidegger suggests that the *ens causa sui* is not a being for whom one would be willing to fall upon one's knees. As we have observed in the preceding section, it is precisely this concept of God as uncaused cause that falls victim to Nietzsche's reverberating proclamation of the death of God, heralding the end of theistic metaphysics. Such a deity, if proven to exist, would indeed be different from any other beings in the vast chain of being. It would not, however, be otherwise than being, for it would remain within the categorial determinations that stimulate the economy of beings.

If talk about God as a being, borrowing the resources of a metaphysics of theism, comes up short both on the philosophical and theological sides of the ledger, might it be that the meaning of divinity could be rescued with the grammar of fundamental ontology? Ontic analysis delivers a concept of God that remains philosophically problematic and theologically idolatrous. Might ontological analysis, however, prove a more trustworthy strategy at that very juncture where ontic analysis fails? Will a shift from an interrogation of the "meaning" of Being within the ontic-ontological difference to the "truth" of Being put us on more substantial terrain in pursuing the question about God?

It would seem that in Heidegger's "Letter on Humanism" an invitation to link the elucidation of the truth of Being to the question about the Deity is extended. There we are told that it is only from the vantage point of the truth of Being that the essence of the holy and divinity can be thought, in light of which the meaning of the word *God* achieves its proper signification. It were as though Paul Tillich, Heidegger's colleague at Marburg University in the 1920s, accepted the invitation to appropriate Heidegger's fundamental ontology in designing his *Systematic Theology*. In this work we find Tillich's most explicit references to God as

"Being-itself," the "Ground of Being," and the "Power of Being." It would thus seem that in Tillich's project of "transcending theism," with the move to the "God Above God" as elaborated in *The Courage To Be*, we have left the classical metaphysical concept of God behind, but we have still retained the resources of fundamental ontology in our discourse about the divine.

Might it be that Tillich, in what appears to be a hurried embrace of the ontological grammar of Heidegger II in his readiness to speak of God as Being-itself, has neglected to consider the hermeneutical shift from Heidegger II to Heidegger III? Matters become more interesting, but also more complex, in the move to what in a previous work we have named the "*second* turning" in Heidegger's thought. This second turning marks the shift to Heidegger III, following in the wake of the first turning, namely from Heidegger I (the meaning of Being) to Heidegger II (the truth of Being). In Heidegger III the shift is even more pronounced than that which characterizes the first turning. Here there is a move away from the Being-problem itself, which results not only in a delimitation of the ontic/ontological difference that guided Heidegger's explorations in *Being and Time* but a veritable rupture of philosophical inquiry, a *coupure philosophique*, derailing the inquiry that seeks to solve the problem of Being. The new space that is opened as a result of this second turning is the space marked out by the "erasure of Being"—the "crossing out" (*Durchstreichung*) of Being is the way Heidegger expresses it in *Zur Seinsfrage*.[37]

What is the relevance of this second turning in the thought of Heidegger for the task of theology and the question about God? Is this second turning, announcing the erasure, or crossing out, of Being, to be understood as a postmodern avatar of Plato's otherwise than being? And if so, might this provide for an opening of a new perspective on the God-question? Might this move beyond the economy of beings (*Seiendes*) as well as the ontological site of Being (*Sein*) provide instruction on the meaning and use of a transcendence that in the accentuated hyperbole of Levinas is other than the other? Before hastily appropriating Heidegger's crossing out of Being as a possible theme for theological inquiry and thus avoiding what may have been a problem in Tillich's hurried appropriation of Heidegger's fundamental ontology, it would be wise to give some studied attention to what precisely is entailed by Heidegger's move to erase the word *Being* in our philosophical conversations and its potential for theological understanding. The jury is apparently still out

---

37. Heidegger, *Zur Seinsfrage*, 30–35. For an extended discussion of the hermeneutical profiles of I, II, and III in Heidegger's reflections on the problem of Being and beyond, see Schrag, "The Three Heideggers," 159–73.

on this issue. Derrida, for example, is not convinced that *Being* suffers all that much of an erasure, even in Heidegger's later thought. After having been subjected to a crossing out, muses Derrida, "The word *being* is not avoided; it remains readable." Avoidance is not its essential function. Indeed, in the end the crossing out of Being carries a positive signification. It discloses the nonobjectifiable discourse about the fourfold (*Geviert*), in which earth and heavens, mortals and the divine, come to presence in a unifying poetic vision.[38]

The erasure of Being in Heidegger III can thus be seen as an invitation to poetic thinking and dwelling, of which indeed much is made in the later Heidegger. Poetic thinking commemorates rather than represents; it proceeds by way of showing rather than referring, it is a setting forth instead of an explaining, and it is evocative rather than demonstrative.[39] The language that always accompanies poetic thinking is the performance of "saying" (*Sagen*), the narrating of a story of our caring for the earth, our sojourn as mortals, and our yearning for the gods. There is here a decisive rupture both with the epistemological grammar of referring and the semiotic construal of language as a system of signs. This shift from the thinking and speaking under the aegis of the meaning of Being (Heidegger I) and the truth of Being (Heidegger II) to the poetic thinking and saying under the aegis of the crossing out of Being (Heidegger III) requires a substitution of the vocabulary of Being for the vocabulary of event of appropriation (*Ereignis*).[40]

The second turning, the erasure of Being in the thought of Heidegger, has thus brought us to a critical juncture. Indeed, it has brought us

38. "If this *Durchstreichung* is neither a sign nor merely a negative sign (*'kein bloss negatives Zeichen'*), this is because it does not efface 'Being' beneath conventional and abstract marks. Heidegger understands it as showing (*zeigen*) the four regions (*Gegenden*) of what he here and elsewhere calls the fourfold (*Geviert*): earth and heavens, mortals and the divine," Derrida, "How to Avoid Speaking: Denials," 125.

39. The grammar of "setting forth" and "evocation" that informs poetic thinking also recalls the epideictic function of rhetoric as it was defined by the ancients. *Epi-deixis* is precisely a disclosing, evoking, showing, and setting forth. Thus, the requirement becomes that of recognizing the entwinement of poetical and rhetorical thinking in the later philosophy of Heidegger. Michael J. Hyde has addressed this entwinement in his essay "Rhetorically Man Dwells: On the Making-known Function of Discourse," *Communication* 7 (1983), 201–20. Also, see his book *The Call of Conscience: Heidegger and Levinas, Rhetoric and the Euthanasia Debate* (Columbia: University of South Carolina Press, 2001), where he elucidates the call of conscience in the thought of Heidegger and Levinas as illustrating an epideictic function of evoking and setting forth a rhetorical interruption as it pertains specifically to the soul-wrenching decision making in regards to euthanasia.

40. Schrag, "The Three Heideggers," 172.

to the "end of philosophy." We are now in the region of poetic thinking, saying, and dwelling, and find ourselves speaking about the event of appropriation rather than Being. But have we come any closer to addressing the question about God? Are we now on the threshold of getting a glimpse of the Deity as otherwise than Being? One does well to tread with some caution at this juncture and heed the caveat issued by Heidegger himself in his response to the query about his linking of the truth of Being to the signification of the word *God* in his "Letter on Humanism." He replied: "With respect to the text referred to from the 'Letter on Humanism,' what is being discussed there is the God of the poet, not the revealed God."[41] On more than one occasion Heidegger informed his listeners and readers that were he to write a work on theology, the word *Being* would not appear—apparently not even under erasure! He has not written such a work. Had he done so, we would need to find a space for Heidegger IV, in which would occur a shift from the elucidations of the God of the poet to attestations of the God of revealed theology and religious experience.

In a retrospective glance over our preceding discussions, reviewing the progression of topics that we have pursued, we recall that we began examining the entanglement of the problem of being and the question about God and the resultant vagaries in the annals of classical theism. Joining forces with metaphysics as the science of beings, classical theism was destined to define God as a being among other beings. Admittedly God was assigned a space on the highest rung in the scale of beings— prime mover, first cause, necessary being, a supernatural entity infinite and perfect. Yet, even as the highest and most exemplary being, God remained within the economy of relations of substance and attribute and cause and effect. Not only did this threaten his alleged transcendence, but it rendered problematic his religious significance for the stages along life's way.

For a time, however, sticking with the problem of being, we held out some hope that fundamental ontology might help get matters straight on the true nature and dynamics of the Deity. But this hope also remained unfulfilled as we encountered the erasure of Being and learned that the most the poetic thinking that accompanies this erasure could achieve was the disclosure of the gods of the poet and their manifestations as a presence within the fourfold of earth and sky, mortals and the divine. What would appear to be required at this juncture is a new semantics—

---

41. Heidegger, "Appendix," *The Piety of Thinking,* 65.

a semantics that resides outside of the "house of Being." The semantics of Heidegger II, which propels one beyond language as an articulation of the structures of *Dasein* (Heidegger I) to the veritable edifice of Being, can only speak of the deities from a poetical perspective. We are thus invited, as we approach part 2 of the present study, to examine the possibility of a robust and hyperbolic transcendence that would at once proceed beyond the concept of God fettered by the categories of metaphysics, the concept of God as framed by a fundamental ontology, and the role of the deities in poetic thinking and dwelling. We thus seem veritably to have come to the "end of philosophy" in our pursuit of the question about God.

If the conversation about God as truly otherwise than a grammar of beings and Being, outside the economy not only of metaphysical and ontological reflection but also that of the poetic imagination, is to continue, we will need to maneuver a semantic shift in our discourse about the Deity. Levinas on this particular issue may turn out to be more helpful than most. His transposition of transcendence from an ontological into an ethical key opens new possibilities for thinking about God as the other than the other. Levinas is of the mind that if we are going to achieve some clarity on what is at issue in the understanding of transcendence as it applies to the Deity, we will need to turn our attention away from ontology to the ethical: "Transcendence is ethical, and the subjectivity which in the final analysis is not the 'I think' (which it is at first sight), or the unity of the 'transcendental apperception,' is, as responsibility for the other, subjection to the other."[42] And the domain of the ethical, Levinas insists, is not to be found within the domain of the ontological. "Ethics is not a moment of being, it is otherwise and better than being: the very possibility of the beyond."[43]

In one stroke, as it were, Levinas undermines the metaphysical, the ontological, the transcendental, and the existential notions of transcendence and recommends that we explore the meaning of transcendence as an event of the ethical. Among other things, this invites us to consider responsibility as the decisive moment of the ethical. Admittedly, what Levinas understands by "ethics" may not be wholly unproblematic, but his recommendation that we be done with an ontology of presence in think-

42. Levinas, *Of God Who Comes to Mind*, 68.
43. Ibid., 69; cf. 108: "The transcendence toward God is neither linear like the focus of intentionality nor teleological so as to end at the punctuality of a pole and thus stop at beings and substantives. Neither is it even initially dialogical, naming a 'you' (*tu*). Is this transcendence toward God not already produced by ethical transcendence, so that desire and love might be made more perfect than satisfaction?"

ing and speaking about God merits careful consideration. Our response
to this recommendation will take the form of a thought experiment that
involves a shift away from God-talk itself, an overture to a new grammar
and a new semantics, accompanied by a new hermeneutics of praxis,
all of which will revolve around an acknowledgment of and response to
"the Gift."

PART 2

GOD AND THE GIFT

3

From Ontology to Ethics

The Delimitation of Presence

The conjunction of the grammars of being and presence has determined philosophical inquiry from the ancients to recent times. The presupposition that "to be" is in some sense "to be present" informed the *eidos* of Plato, the *ousia* of Aristotle, the *ens causa sui* of the medievals, the cogito of Descartes, the infinite substance of Spinoza, the sense impressions of Hume, the transcendental ego of Kant, and the intentionality of consciousness in the phenomenology of Husserl.

It is a defining mark of postmodernity to call into question the privileging of presence and its conjunction with being. The strident problematization by Heidegger and Derrida of the received metaphysics of presence is very much an integral feature of the postmodern challenge. It is the central point of contention in Heidegger's distinction between the ontic constructionism of metaphysics and the ontological analytic of fundamental ontology. The planking of categories in the interests of securing a representation of the totality of beings as entities present in their standing-within-themselves, rooted in a selfsame substantiality, is precisely what needs to be subject to an *Abbau*, a deconstruction, wherewith to open a path to an understanding of the meaning and truth of Being as an ever coming-to-presence (*Anwesenheit*). Herein resides the moral in the story of the stultifying effects of a metaphysics of presence and the liberating possibilities in an ontological refiguration of presence. It would appear that Heidegger's ontological turn heralds a recovery of sorts, a retrieval of a sense of presence that has been occluded by metaphysical constructionism. After the metaphysics of presence is deconstructed, a new notion of presence comes into view. The presence of entities being on-hand (*Vorhandensein*) is rethought and reanalyzed into coming-to-presence as event or happening. Heidegger's project of deconstruction remains that of a "deconstructive retrieval." And it is this that supplies the bone of contention in the thought of Heidegger's left-wing followers, of whom Derrida remains the most representative.

Derrida is of the mind that in Heidegger's distinction between a metaphysics of presence and an ontology of coming-to-presence the one can easily stand in for the other, and that if we are indeed prepared to take the strategy of deconstruction seriously there will in the end be little, if anything, to retrieve. Derrida surely has Heidegger in mind when he sorts out the two meanings of deconstruction, the one "a deconstruction without changing the terrain, by repeating what is implicit in the founding concepts and the original problematic" and the other a form of deconstruction that makes an effort "to change terrain, in a discontinuous and irruptive fashion, by brutally placing oneself outside, and by affirming an absolute break and difference."[1] Although Derrida is willing to grant that these are distinguishable types of deconstruction that tend to slide into each other, his predilection is toward the latter, a more Nietzschean than Heideggerian strategy.

However, the family dispute between Heidegger and Derrida with regard to the particular advantage of the one or the other kind of deconstruction is overshadowed by subsequent hermeneutical shifts in the pursuit of their related projects. In the case of Heidegger, we observe a shift from the question as to the truth of Being to an erasure or crossing out of Being, in a move to *Ereignis* as an event of appropriation that lies beyond the horizon of the ontic-ontological difference. In the case of Derrida, we are able to observe an amendment, if not a revision, of his earlier stance on the uses of deconstruction. Replying to Jean-Luc Nancy's query, "Who comes after the subject?" Derrida muses: "What are we aiming at in the deconstructions of the 'subject' when we ask ourselves what, in the structure of the classical subject, continues to be required by the question 'Who?' . . . I would add something that remains required by both the definitions of the classical subject and by these later nonclassical motifs, namely a certain responsibility."[2] In this appeal to the grammar of event and appropriation in the later Heidegger and in the appeal to responsibility in the later Derrida, we appear to be thrust into another space, a space of an "ethic," or more precisely a "protoethic," that is in some manner otherwise than Being. And in the ruminations by Derrida in particular, a gesture to his former mentor, Emmanuel Levinas, would seem at this stage to become rather pronounced.

1. Jacques Derrida, "The Ends of Man," in *Margins of Philosophy,* trans. Alan Bass (Chicago: University of Chicago Press, 1982), 135.

2. Eduardo Cadava, Peter Connor, and Jean-Luc Nancy, eds., *Who Comes after the Subject?* (New York: Routledge, 1991), 100.

That allusions to the delimitation of the Being problematic in the later reflections of Heidegger and particularly within the writings of the later Derrida should occasion a reference to Levinas is not all that surprising. It were as though ruminations on the crossing out of Being by Heidegger, and the reconstitution of the subject as responsibility by Derrida, finds its fulfillment in Levinas's attestation of that which is otherwise than being and in his recommendation for an "ethic of responsibility."

Levinas, however, begins his critique of ontology through a critical engagement with Husserl. Profoundly respectful of Husserl's accomplishments as the father of phenomenology, Levinas nonetheless finds it necessary to think *against* him in the process of thinking *with* him. Like Hume, who with his philosophical skepticism awakened Kant from his dogmatic slumbers, so Husserl provided the stimulus for an awakening on the part of Levinas. "Husserl's transcendental reduction," observes Levinas, "has, as its vocation, to awaken the I from numbness, to reanimate its life and its horizons lost in anonymity." This awakening follows the dynamics of a progression "from consciousness to wakefulness"—a wakefulness that, Levinas emphasizes, "is a wakefulness without intentionality . . . without intentionality, otherwise than being."[3]

Such an awakening is required because of the bugbear of presence that travels with Husserl's concept of intentional consciousness. Consciousness as intentional from bottom up, according to Husserl, is always a consciousness *of* . . . of a *cogitatum* that defines the intended object given to consciousness, first in its presentational immediacy and then in its representational ideality. This is the truth of Husserl's objective reduction, securing the status of the presence of the object-as-meant. The subjective reduction follows on the heels of the objective reduction, traversing the circuit of a self-reflexivity whereby the cogito as the intentional act achieves knowledge of the ego as source of all intentional consciousness. This is the truth garnered by the subjective reduction, securing the presence of an ego, transcendental in character, as the ground of all representations.

It is, however, the intersubjective reduction in Husserl's programmatic that elicits Levinas's primary interest, for it is here the issue of the other becomes unavoidable. It is the phenomenon of alterity, the other's showing of himself or herself, that unsettles the presence of an ego serenely present to itself in its unperturbed self-identity. "The intersubjective reduction, starting from the other (*l'autre*), will tear the I out of its coincidence with self and with the center of the world, even if

3. Levinas, *Of God Who Comes to Mind*, 26.

Husserl never ceases, for all that, to think about the relationship between me and the other in terms of knowledge."[4] It was the genius of Husserl, in the "Fifth Meditation" of his *Cartesian Meditations,* to acknowledge the impingement of the other within the structure of transcendental intersubjectivity. His shortcoming was to continue "to think about the relationship between me and the other in terms of knowledge," and by this we are to understand "knowledge" in terms of a representational theory of knowledge that issues from a centered and self-identical ego bent upon the recovery of a pure presence.

It is thus the dynamics activated in the move from consciousness to wakefulness that entail a profound delimitation of presence—both the presence of the object of intentional consciousness and the presence of the subject of consciousness. But this is not the final end or goal of the awakening. The envisioned goal is the acknowledgment and realization of the ethical demand. And we are reminded time and again that ethics is not to be subsumed under ontology. Ethics is not a moment of being. The space of ethics lies beyond the ontological quest. I experience the ethical demand in confronting the other; more precisely stated, the call to ethical responsibility surges up when the other confronts me. And the other resists reduction to an object of intentional consciousness, an other-for-me, an alter ego the meaning of which is conferred through the workings of a constituting consciousness.

The ethical move beyond ontology opens the self to responsibility. Subjectivity becomes translated into responsibility to and for the other. "Transcendence is ethical," reiterates Levinas, "and the subjectivity which in the final analysis is not the 'I think' (which it is at first sight), or the unity of the 'transcendental apperception,' is, as responsibility for the other, subjection to the other."[5] After the subjectivity that defines the presence of the "I think," either in Cartesian or Kantian dress, and the presence of the unity of apperception, either in a Kantian or Husserlian mode, has been duly delimited, a new texture of subjectivity appears on the horizon. This is a subjectivity that takes on the lineament of responsibility. It is important at this juncture to note that "the subject" and "subjectivity" have not been removed from the philosophical lexicon. It is rather that they are refigured against the backdrop of their insertion into the density of ethical existence. And this refiguration of subjectivity within the ethical domain redefines the subject in terms of its responsibility in a "subjection" to the other. No longer a sovereign and autonomous ethical subject, affirming its rights and privileges as an

4. Ibid., 26.
5. Ibid., 68.

independent moral entity, the subject is transvalued into a responsibility to and for the other. It would appear that it is precisely such a refiguration of subjectivity, instead of an elimination of it, that is at issue in Derrida's portrait of the "Who" that retains an existential interest in the classical and nonclassical definitions of the subject in the wake of their deconstruction.

The end run by Derrida and Levinas around Husserl's constituting consciousness and transcendental subjectivity should not, however, be construed as a simple inversion of the vectors of intentionality. More is required than a rewriting of Husserl's "Fifth Meditation" in such a manner that intentionality would move from the other to the ego-cogito. This would not do, for then the ego, the subject, would remain within the schema of representation as the object-as-meant from the vantage point of the other. To be sure, the face of the other is never an identifiable phenomenon in the guise of an intended *noema* or *cogitatum* constituted by an intending *noesis* or *cogito;* but neither is the subject of ethical responsibility an object-as-meant for a commanding other. A more radical move beyond the framework of intentional analysis is required. The intentionality of constituting consciousness still proceeds against the backdrop of the subject-object dichotomy in the classical epistemology of recognition and representation, condemning both self and other to a fate of objectivization. The continued use of the framework of intentional analysis and constitution becomes particularly pernicious when we are taught, as we are by Levinas, to seek God as Wholly Other, in the face of the neighbor. When God becomes an object for an existing subject, the effacement of his divinity is threatened by a species of conceptual idolatry; when we become objects for God's vision, his divinity is again threatened with a reduction to tyrannical control and our subjectivity is divested of all personal freedom as a condition for responsibility.

The delimitation of the presence that is presupposed in the *re*presentation of the signified content, the object of intentional consciousness, invites an experimentation with a new grammar. The new grammar that has been provided by Levinas and Derrida is the grammar of the "trace." The trace surpasses, if not displaces, the sign. The trace becomes the true bearer of meaning. It is still a matter of meaning, but apparently no longer a matter of *signitive* meaning. There is a meaning that comes to expression in the face that is older than the meaning that is comported by the sign. The face, says Levinas, is "the latent birth of meaning."[6] But this meaning as trace antedates the event of signification, or to enunciate

6. Ibid., 168.

the point in a more paradoxical register, "The beyond from which a face comes signifies as a trace."[7]

What the peculiar consequences of Levinas's shift of grammar from sign to trace are is not all that easy to sort out. Initially there is the ambiguity in the surpassing of the sign by the trace. Does the trace simply and straightforwardly displace the sign? Does it supplement it? Is the trace to be grafted onto the workings of the sign? Does it somehow complete the function of signification? Are we to situate a hermeneutic of the trace alongside an epistemology of recognition and representation? Is a trace once and for all done with matters of presence? Apparently a trace is not a mark, token, vestige, or intimation of a *lost* presence, which somehow might be reclaimed. This would be to fall back upon the exhausted resources of a doctrine of recollection. But might it possibly be an announcement of a presence yet to come? Or perchance is it a token of a presence always deferred, always in the future, residing in a space that will never become present?

What manner of presence (or nonpresence) are we to ascribe to the dynamics of the trace? This would appear to become a matter of crucial interest when the face of the neighbor as trace exhibits the alterity of the divine as Infinite and Wholly Other. Somewhat enigmatically, Levinas frames the issue as follows: "We think that the idea-of-the Infinite-in-me— or my relation to God—comes to me in the concreteness of my relation to the other person, in the sociality which is my responsibility for the neighbor."[8] In what manner does the Infinite "come to me" as a trace in the face of my neighbor? In what manner is the face of my neighbor present? In what manner is God present in the face of my neighbor? Admittedly, the notion of presence at issue here is neither that of a metaphysical substrate nor of an epistemological condition, but it would appear that some sense of presence remains operative. The "problem" of presence does not seem to vanish in the aftermath of its delimitation as either a metaphysical or an epistemological protocol.

The Ethical and the Sacramental

The shift from ontology to ethics needs to be coordinated with a new perspective on the meaning of presence. The face of the other as the origin

---

7. Emmanuel Levinas, "The Trace of the Other," in *Deconstruction in Context: Literature and Philosophy,* ed. Mark C. Taylor (Chicago: University of Chicago Press, 1986), 355.

8. Emmanuel Levinas, *Time and the Other and Additional Essays,* trans. Richard A. Cohen (Pittsburgh: Duquesne University Press, 1987), 136.

of the ethical and the accompanying disclosure of the Deity as absolute alterity in the face of the other, both in some manner come to presence in the ethical requirement. But in what sense come to presence? To be sure, always coming to presence only as *trace* and not as objectifiable referent. But even a trace, to retain any degree of intelligibility, needs to make some manner of appearance on the ethical scene. The trace of the other in the face of the neighbor, the stranger, the widow, and the orphan is imbued with the temporality of commemoration, whereas the absolute alterity of the divine in the face of the other is immemorial. Whence and in what manner is the presence of the immemorial in the temporal? And in what sense immemorial and in what sense temporal? These are matters all very closely entwined, and they need to be sorted out so as to achieve optimal clarity on the elusive figuration of presence in the transactions of ethical responsibility.

In the history of religion, both in the West and in the East, the problem of presence in ethical life has been coupled with the problem of presence in religious places, names, artifacts, rituals, ceremonies, and sacraments. It is here the traditional distinction between the sacred and the secular, the holy and the profane, reaches its most intensive expression. Whether one is dealing with the allegedly sacred properties of the totem animal in totemism, with the sacred cow of Hinduism, with the Holy of Holies that houses the Ark of the Covenant in Judaism, with the name of Allah in Islam, or with the eucharistic elements of the bread and the wine in Christianity, the distinction between the sacred and the secular, the holy and the profane, is in play. The sacred is attested to as becoming in some manner present in an intramundane object. But in what manner present? The problem of presence is thus seen to spill over the edges of both ethical and sacramental practices, and our quandary about how to deal with this perplexing issue becomes intensified.

The issue at stake, as is the case with most of the issues in philosophy and religion, is not of recent date. It came to the fore in the distinction between the prophetic and the priestly functions of religion in ancient times. The functions of the prophet and the priest in world religions have always been rather clearly distinguished. Prophets accentuate the ethical side of religion; priests emphasize the ceremonial and sacramental functions of religious practices. The prophetic orientation tends to be radical with respect to the status quo, often iconoclastic in nature, geared to initiatives of social reform; the priestly orientation is conservative by disposition, holding on to that which is deemed to be good by the tradition, with a heavy investment in the economy of icons. Prophets, although they address their hearers in the name of a transcending reality (and thus need to be distinguished from cultural critics within the economy of civil society), nonetheless understand their leadership roles in terms of a vocation, a "calling," to serve humankind independent of any specific ecclesiastical sanctions. Priests, on the other hand, have conferred upon them the mandate of authority, issuing from an office within an ecclesiastical structure.

A classic illustration of the prophetic function of religion is that of the prophets of ancient Israel of the eighth century B.C. "I hate, I despise your feasts," writes the prophet Amos. "Yea, though ye offer me your burnt offerings and meal offerings, I will not accept them; . . . Take thou away from me the noise of thy songs; . . . but let justice roll down as waters, and righteousness as a mighty stream."[9] The prophetic motif of the priority of justice and the hollowness of ceremonial practices emerges here with unmistakable clarity. The prophetic denunciation of the ceremonial in the interests of societal reform based on justice is continued in the voice of the prophet Hosea when he urges his hearers to make a covenant with Jehovah "in righteousness, and in justice, and in loving-kindness, and in mercies."[10] Here we note that justice is coupled with loving-kindness and mercy. In the Book of Micah we find a striking consummate formulation of the prophetic principle, interweaving the requirements for justice, mercy, and humility: "What doth Jehovah require of thee, but to do justly, and to love kindness, and to walk humbly with thy God?"[11]

The tension between the prophetic and priestly functions of religion was a distinguishing feature of the Judaic tradition, as it was also of Christianity and Islam, suggesting that the tension may well be an endemic feature of religion more generally. In Christianity the tension is discernible in the institutional differences between Catholicism and Protestantism—particularly among the left-wing, radical Protestant reformers of the Anabaptist tradition, who had little use for the priestly role and its heavy investment in the sacramental. The prophetic/ethical and priestly/sacramental functions of religion would thus appear to be orthogonal to institutional practices across the spectrum of world religions. Our particular interest in this division of functions has to do with the claims for a presence of the Deity in each.

The primacy of the ethical in the approach of Levinas is particularly illustrative of a latter-day prophetic orientation. In moving from ontology to ethics, Levinas becomes a veritable witness to the prophetic call for justice, loving-kindness, and mercy. But he leaves us with a problem in

9. Amos, 5.21–24 ASV.
10. Hosea 2.19 ASV.
11. Micah 6.8 ASV.

dealing with the phenomenon of ethical presence after the traditional ontological fabrications of presence are jettisoned. In what manner does the self experience presence in responding to the call of the other, and in what manner is God present in the face of the stranger, the widow, and the orphan? If we are going to speak of an ethic of responsibility—at once responsibility to the neighbor and to God—we will need to recognize a "responding center" that identifies the presence from which one's responsive thought and action proceeds, as well as a "soliciting presentment" that issues from the face and the voice of the other.

The lamenting of the co-opting of this responding center and soliciting presentment by the traditional metaphysics of presence, which dissects everything into polarizing opposites (substance/attribute, subject/object, essence/existence, form/matter, actuality/potentiality, activity/passivity), has become a popular pastime, which admittedly has its own rewards. We have much to learn from Levinas's repeated reminder that the passivity of the ethical self in its asymmetrical relation with the face of the other is "a passivity more passive than any passivity appropriate to a consciousness."[12] The metaphysical constructs of an active and a passive voice, an independent initiating agent and a dependent receiving patient, have pretty much outworn their usefulness. What is required is a new perspective on the coming to presence of self and other in the ethical relation.

If the vocabularies of presence and self-identity are to continue to service our philosophical needs in getting clear about the status of the ethical subject, we will have to distinguish the ethical posture on presence and self-identity from their metaphysical constructs. The presence of the ethical subject in the acknowledgment of its responsibility to the face and voice of the other is not the presence of an entity congealed into an elusive now-point as an instant of time; and the self-identity of the ethical subject is not that legislated by the objectivating criteria of identification, geared to a definition of the subject as somehow fixed and finished, immune to all change, insulated from the ravages of time. The uses of such objectivating criteria, dear to the heart of traditional metaphysicians, places the identity of the self outside of time, inviting a rather peculiar state of affairs in which the subject is removed from the temporal register.

The presence and self-identity of the ethical subject, unlike that appealed to in dealing with matters of quantity and number, is a presence and self-identity embedded within the temporal becoming of the

12. Levinas, *Of God Who Comes to Mind,* 64.

self, occasioning an experience of presence borne by a remembrance of that which has been and an anticipation of that which is yet to come. Temporality enters into the very constitution of the ethical subject. The main point at issue here is that the self-identity of the ethical subject is a *personal* identity. However, it is not a personal identity extracted from its social milieu. It is an identity within the interstices of the subject's personal and social development. It is the identity of the "character" in the story of the subject as sojourner across the changing landscapes of human existence. Hence, it is appropriate to speak of the personal identity of the ethical subject as a "narrative identity," distinguishing it from relations of number and quantity at issue in the identification of entities that make up the world of objects and things.

In seeking clarification on the distinguishing feature of the self-identity of the ethical subject, we still have much to learn from Kierkegaard's penetrating elucidation of the ethical existence-sphere as one of the three "stages on life's way." The pivotal mark of ethical existence, as understood by Kierkegaard, is the achievement of existential continuity. "Self-constancy" becomes the hallmark of the self-identity of the ethical subject. This achievement of self-constancy requires a new attitude toward temporality. The present is no longer viewed as a transient erotic instant, as it is for the aesthete. The present takes on the texture of an "opportune moment," providing the concrete coordinate of lived time and lived space as the vicinity for existential choice. Ethical life for Kierkegaard is the life of decision and commitment. And it is in this call to commitment that the self-constancy of the ethical subject is achieved. But this self-constancy is not riveted in an abstract serialized instant; it provides the space for the present as a moment that contains within itself both the past and the future.

As the present of ethical time is not an isolated now, so the past is not a succession of instants that have gone by and are to be forgotten. Such is precisely the life of the aesthete, in which the past is a series of erotic instants that are to be forgotten as the aesthete searches for a new erotic instant to fill the void. In the life of the ethical subject, the past is constitutive of the life of the self, holding previous decisions, which need to be revalued time and again.

Likewise, the future for the ethical subject is not a series of nows that are not yet real. The future is the horizon of self-actualization that marks out the region of existential possibilities. The future is constitutive of selfhood, constituting the self as open to choices yet to be made. The soul of the ethical subject, Judge William announces in *Either/Or,* is "matured in the hour of decision," in which the ethical subject "chooses himself as a concretion determined in manifold ways, and he chooses himself therefore in accord with his continuity."[13] Kierkegaard's redescription of personal self-identity as self-constancy provides a window of opportunity for viewing the transition from metaphysical to ethical self-identity. The ethical subject is a subject that is present to itself both in its memory and in its hope. A self that has nothing to remember and nothing for which to hope is a self bereft of ethical substance.

Some such redescription of the presence and self-identity of the ethical subject as offered by Kierkegaard is needed to determine the responding center in the ethical transaction. But there is yet to be determined the presence and identity of the soliciting presentment of the face and voice of the other. And this is a particularly demanding requirement if, as Levinas avers, it is precisely the absolute alterity of God that "comes to mind" in the visage and cries of the widow, the orphan, and the stranger. In the thought of Levinas, the alterity of God extends the trace in the face of the neighbor to its farthest horizon. God is manifest, "comes to mind," in the visage of the other person. As noted, for Levinas, my relation to God "comes to me in the concreteness of my relation to the other person." But what is the soliciting presentment that becomes manifest and comes to mind? What sort of presence or identity can be ascribed to God? Clearly, the presence at issue cannot be the presence of an entity congealed into an instant of time. It is an "immemorial" present, outside the economy of temporal succession and simultaneity. If the vocabulary of presence still has utility in speaking of God, then one would need to describe it as an omnipresence, transcending the temporal manifold but still somehow efficacious within it.

At this juncture, the lure of negative theology appears virtually irresistible. Why not a bold-faced admission that positive knowledge of the presence of the Deity is inaccessible for the finite human mind and that one can only say what God is not? But this route is as unacceptable for Levinas as it is for us. The play with the "is" and the "is not" in negative theology remains within the economy of being/nonbeing, and it is precisely from this we were to be liberated in the move from ontology to ethics. The ontological problematic in negative theology is compounded with a semantic and epistemological problematic. Such was already foreshadowed in the title of the main work by Pseudo-Dionysus, *On Divine Names*. Set within the framework of a search for the proper names of the Deity, negative theology is unable to avoid the semantic and epistemological quandaries of an undecidability of meaning and

---

13. Søren Kierkegaard, *Either/Or: A Fragment of Life*, trans. Walter Lowrie (Princeton, N.J.: Princeton University Press, 1949), 2: 133, 211.

indeterminacy of reference. What is required is a shift of focus away from a preoccupation with naming to the disclosing function of narration. Names will indeed continue to play a role in our discourse about both our neighbor and our God, but names do not comport meaning in and of themselves, decontextualized from the stories that we tell about the entwined discourse and action that make up the fabric of our communicative praxis. The meaning of the presence of the Deity cannot be captured in an exercise of trying to find the right name. It requires a broader context of considerations of narrative as a form of life. And within this broader context of considerations the question of how the presence of the Deity emerges against the backdrop of the move from ontology to ethics still awaits an answer.

There are some intermittent suggestions in the writings of Levinas that point in the direction of an answer to this perplexing question. In *Time and the Other*, for example, Levinas refers to Henri Bergson's notion of the élan vital as that which "signifies love of the neighbor and what I have called 'to-God.' "[14] And in the same work we read: "Responsibility is without concern for reciprocity: I have to respond to and for the Other without occupying myself with the Other's responsibility in my regard. A relationship without correlation, love of the neighbor is love without eros. It is for-the-other-person and, through this, to-God!"[15] The ethical presence of God is manifested, comes to mind, in the love of the neighbor; and this, Levinas emphasizes, is a love to be understood as nonreciprocal, distinct from eros, which is a love that is always conditional and expects something in return.

In moving from ethical presence to sacramental presence, from the prophetic vision to the priestly ceremonial, we revisit our quandaries with the problem of presence. How is the divine and the holy present in the ritual performance of the sacraments? An object or event is considered to be sacramental under the condition that the transcendent Wholly Other is deemed in some fashion to be present. But again, in what sense present? Not only did the priestly function of religion, with its privileging of the ceremonial, occasion the prophetic protests of the eighth-century prophets of ancient Israel, the sacramental system of medieval Catholicism collided with the protesting principle of the sixteenth-century Protestant Reformation. It is precisely on this issue that the split between Catholicism and Protestantism became most visible. The Protestant reformers, who were intent on ferreting out idolatries in every nook

14. Levinas, *Time and the Other*, 120.
15. Ibid., 137.

and cranny, were quick to land upon the sacramental claims for an objective presence of the divine in the physical elements of bread and wine as yet another illustration of widespread idolatrous tendencies in the medieval church.

One of the more provocative (in the sense of thought-provoking) efforts to rescue a viable notion of sacramental presence that might avoid the snares of idolatry is that provided by Jean-Luc Marion in his notion of a "eucharistic hermeneutics" that is at the center of "the eucharistic site of theology." Marion's concern is to bridge the hermeneutic of the preachment of the Word with the hermeneutic of the performance of the Eucharist. This can be accomplished successfully, he maintains, only when one recognizes that "the Eucharist alone completes the hermeneutic; the hermeneutic culminates in the Eucharist," based on the conditional, "If the Word intervenes in person only at the eucharistic moment, *the hermeneutic (hence fundamental theology) will take place, will have its place, only in the Eucharist.*"[16]

Marion stands ready to underscore the crucial, indeed pivotal, role of the Eucharist in matters theological. Yet, in seeking to work out an understanding of the presence in the sacramental ritual, Marion wants to avoid the idolatry that has traveled with the traditional theological doctrine of transubstantiation, which gravitates toward a sacramental chemistry that construes the presence of the holy as resident in the intramundane objects of the bread and the wine. The presence at issue is not the presence of a something within another something. Considered as such it would catapult us into an idolatry of a represented object.

However, the jettisoning of the metaphysical trappings of the doctrine of transubstantiation does not, according to Marion, entail a jettisoning of all senses of presence. One need, however, he insists, be on guard against simply shifting the locus of presence to another idol— for example, the consciousness and state of mind of the participating individual and the community. The reduction of the eucharistic presence to the consciousness of the worshipper, or indeed that of the community, is simply another form of idolatry: "The absence of a represented object hence does not eliminate idolatry, but establishes the coming to immediate consciousness of eucharistic presence as the insurmountable idol."[17] We are therefore enjoined to think eucharistic presence without lapsing into idolatry. But how is this to be accomplished? We seem to be caught in the double bind of gravitating either toward a species of

16. Marion, *God without Being*, 150–51.
17. Ibid., 169.

objective realism or that of subjective idealism. Either the presence is in the "thing," the physical elements of bread and wine with their distinctive chemical properties, or it is in the mind of the believer. How might one escape this double bind without losing any and all senses of presence? Marion suggests that this could be achieved by focusing on the eucharistic presence as indeed having its locus in the "present," but the present understood as a gift. "One must measure the dimensions of eucharistic presence against the fullness of this gift. . . . *the eucharistic present is deduced from the commitment of charity.*"[18]

In the move from the metaphysical grammar of transubstantiation on the one hand and the privileging of the event of consciousness, individual and communal, on the other hand to the grammar of gift and charity we appear to be approaching a new semantic horizon. Presence-talk would seem to be amenable to analysis into gift-talk. But how does gift-talk as it relates to the Eucharist avoid the snares of idolatry? To answer this question one needs to recall Marion's distinction between an icon and an idol as this distinction plays within the division of the visible and the invisible. An idol is unable to surpass the visible in its effort to reach the invisible. It is self-reflexive, more like a mirror than like a prism, reflecting the image of the gaze rather than permitting the invisible, the divine, to become manifest in it. "The idol consigns the divine to the measure of a human gaze," Marion states, and as such is to be distinguished from the icon that finds its measure not in the human gaze but in the divine. "Whereas the idol results from the gaze that aims at it, the icon summons sight in letting the visible . . . be saturated little by little with the invisible."[19]

What one learns from Marion's distinction between the idol and the icon is that an idolatry of the ritual of the Eucharist is avoided to the degree that one finds the measure of presence in the elements beyond the space of the visible. Hence, the task is to secure the iconic function of the elements against any contamination by the idolatric. It soon becomes evident that Marion's semantics of the icon has at least a family resemblance to the use of the semantics of the symbol in religious discourse. Paul Tillich's semantics of the religious symbol is particularly relevant at this juncture. Tillich's doctrine of the symbol is predicated on the distinction between symbols and signs. Symbols and signs have one thing in common. They both point beyond themselves, indicating something other than themselves. This however is the only commonality

18. Ibid., 171, 178.
19. Ibid.,14, 17.

shared by a semantics of the symbol and a semiotics of the sign. Symbols have the power to participate in the reality to which they point, whereas signs do not.

Such is particularly the case with religious symbols. The traffic light is a sign that signals the requirement to stop or the permission to go. It points beyond itself, but it does not disclose a dimension of depth within the structure of human existence that addresses one's ultimate concern. Religious symbols, according to Tillich, are able to do precisely this. They disclose a depth dimension in our ultimate concerns. The symbol of the cross in Christianity, for example, not only points beyond the material out of which it is made, but discloses the realities of suffering and redemption of which the Christian faith testifies. "The language of faith is the language of symbols," and the difficult task, Tillich continues, is to ensure that the content of faith as that which concerns one ultimately, which in the end is named by Tillich the "God Above God" on the hither side of a transcended theism, finds its proper expression through a discernment of "which symbol of ultimacy expresses the ultimate without idolatrous elements."[20]

Both Marion and Tillich are highly sensitive to the threats of idolatry. Marion warns against mistaking the icon for the idol, and Tillich sees the principal threat to religious faith as the misconstruing of its thesaurus of sacred physical and cultural objects as a storehouse of signs bereft of symbolic power. "This whole realm of sacred objects is a treasure of symbols," writes Tillich. "Holy things are not holy in themselves, but they point beyond themselves to the source of all holiness, that which is of ultimate concern. . . . Faith, if it takes its symbols literally, becomes idolatrous."[21]

To what extent, however, Marion and Tillich are able to avoid a reintroduction of idolatry while remaining within an institutionalized theological focus on the issues does appear to pose a problem. Such is particularly the case with Marion's effort to secure "the eucharistic site of theology." After deconstructing the objective realism of presence in the medieval doctrine of transubstantiation and the subjective idealism of presence as an event in the minds of the community of believers, Marion recommends that we consider the gift of charity as the genuine meaning of the eucharistic presence. But we are also informed that this presence becomes efficacious only within the parameters of a quite specifically institutionalized theological site. The hermeneutics of the Eucharist

20. Paul Tillich, *Dynamics of Faith* (New York: Harper and Brothers Publishers, 1957), 42, 47.

21. Ibid., 48, 52.

achieves its fulfillment only in "the place where *theo*logical interpretation can be exercised, thanks to the liturgical service of the theologian par excellence, the bishop." We must therefore conclude, avers Marion, that *"only the bishop merits, in the full sense, the title of theologian. . . .* Without the presiding of the Eucharist, the hermeneutic does not attain the theological site: the Word in person. . . . *The eucharistic present is deduced from the real edification of the ecclesiastical body of Christ."*[22]

It is at this juncture the priestly function of religion as it pertains to the meaning and role of the sacraments subordinates, if not undermines, the prophetic function of religion. We have seen that both functions move in the direction of a semantics of the gift, which might facilitate the articulation of the meaning of ethical and sacramental presence alike. But grounding the efficacy of the eucharistic presence on the theological site of an ecclesiasticism in which the authority is vested in the official clerical status of the celebrant extends an invitation to what in the end may be an even more pernicious idolatry—an *ecclesiastical* idolatry of a historical institution in its manifold functions, an idolatry in which all icons become idols and remain the property only of those who share the same institutionalized beliefs.

The defining moment of the Protestant Reformation was its protest against the absolutizing tendencies of the medieval church as exhibited in its ecclesiastical structure and its doctrine of the sacraments. As an intramundane historical institution, the church along with all other intramundane entities and organizations testifies of its finitude and frailties, and any claim for ultimacy on its part in matters of faith and morals is but another species of idolatry. This defining moment of Protestantism, its iconoclastic principle of protest, was however attenuated, if not straightway abandoned, in the course of the development of the various forms of Protestant orthodoxy. In this development, Protestantism found itself unable to use the Protestant principle against itself as it gravitated toward multiple forms of its own idolatry—absolutizing church doctrines, creeds, scriptures, founders of sects, or ritual practices.

The truth of the sacraments and its tenuous connection with an elusive presence remains one of the more enigmatic truths of institutionalized religion. Although both Catholicism and Protestantism have displayed intermittent hermeneutical insights into the efficacy of the sacraments, neither has been wholly successful in sheltering the sacramental principle from the threats of idolatry. The performance of the sacraments points to the presence of the sacred in the secular. However,

---

22. Marion, *God without Being*, 152, 153, 179.

the difficult requirement and task is to keep this presence from becoming translated into the metaphysics of an infinite and supernatural being descending into a finite and natural world. Reanalyzing the presence of the sacred into the presentment of gifts, as suggested by Marion, is indeed helpful. Things of the world, from a religious perspective, are gifts—tokens and bestowals not to be devalued. The natural kinds of nature are presented for our enjoyment and our care.

This interpretation of the sacramental principle opens the door to a new view of nature. Nature is no longer viewed as having value only through its subjugation to the needs of the human species. It has an integrity of its own, not simply subject to human contrivance and control. It is a gift, donated to the sojourner along life's way, entrusted to the human species for its stewardship. But this truth of the sacramental principle, attesting to the presence of the sacred in the majesty of nature, undermining the metaphysical bifurcation of the sacred and the secular, is all too quickly violated by the recurring insidious intrusions of idolatry within ecclesiastical manifestos.

The history of the tendencies to mount hegemonic and unconditional claims on the part of institutions, religious and otherwise, has taught us a certain vigilance concerning the alleged authorities of civil and ecclesiastical society. And about this vigilance we still have much to learn from the iconoclastic thought of Dostoevsky, Kierkegaard, and Nietzsche. It was Dostoevsky who in "The Grand Inquisitor" testified of the perniciousness of theocratic idolatry in his poignant portrayal of the medieval cardinal as the modern Pilate. It was Kierkegaard who in his piercing satire *Attack upon "Christendom"* apprised us of the rampant confusion of genuine Christianity with a "crew of bishops, deans, and priests" and their cherished "inventory of churches, bells, organs, benches, almsboxes, foot-warmers, tables, hearses, etc."[23] It was Nietzsche who highlighted the feelings of resentment, ill-will, and revenge that made their way into organized religion and through a serendipitous irony transformed the church into the Antichrist.

Presence and Praxis

Our examination of the difficulties in locating the form and function of presence in the exercise of ethical responsibility and in the celebration of

---

23. Søren Kierkegaard, *Attack upon "Christendom," 1954–1855,* trans. Walter Lowrie (Boston: Beacon Press, 1956), 29–30.

sundry ritual performances requires some experimentation with a new vocabulary so as to bring into prominence the site of this quite elusive phenomenon. Having become dissatisfied with the traditional metaphysical and ontological definitions of presence within theistic metaphysics and onto-theology, an effort to elucidate a wider economy in which talk about the presence of the Deity becomes intelligible may well be worth the expenditure of energy.

The economy we have in mind is an economy in which the vocabulary of praxis takes precedence over the vocabulary of being. Maybe this economy of praxis can provide the proper site for the disclosure of presence, both the presence of the self to itself and the presence of that which is other than self. Although the notion of praxis has been with us since the time of the ancients, having its etymological origin in the Greek verb *prasso*, it has suffered the destiny of becoming sharply marked off from theory (*theōria*), relegated to a lower rank, standing in want of justification by theoretical postulates and principles. Praxis fell victim to the epistemological separation of *epistēmē* and *doxa*, permitting praxis to fraternize with *doxa* while being subordinated to the claims of *epistēmē*. In what Husserl named the developing "crisis of the European sciences," *doxa* became increasingly disparaged, prompting him to speak of "the despised doxa" (*die verächtliche Farbung der δοξα*)[24]. This disparagement of *doxa* was a contributing factor in the accelerated advance of Western rationalism and its preoccupation with theory at the expense of the occlusion of the concrete functioning intentionality of pretheoretical world involvements.

In the wake of the increasing dichotomization of theory-grounded *epistēmē* and praxis-oriented *doxa*, the philosophical task adequate to rescuing the European sciences from their gravitation into a conceptual crisis becomes that of dismantling the dichotomy and restoring the full-bodied disclosing power of praxis—a performing and doing that does not have to wait upon the determinations of categorially limned theory to confer upon it an intelligibility. Imbued with its own resources of understanding, older than the intentionality of consciousness structured as an *ego-cogito-cogitatum* complex, praxis comports an indigenous insight and comprehension.

This notion of praxis, which seems to offer some promise as the site of a pretheoretical understanding of presence, is a praxis textured as an amalgam of discourse and action. Praxis is an intercalation of speaking

---

24. Edmund Husserl, *Die Krisis der europäischen Wissenschaften und die transzendentale Phänomenologie*, ed. Walter Biemel (The Hague: M. Nijhoff, 1954), 127.

and doing, discourse and action, language and social practices. It is both linguistic and behavioral, text and texture, at once a narrative and a lived history. And it is all these prior to the split between theory and practice and the consequent relegation of praxis to a lower-order function that is legitimated only when understood as *applied* theory. The internal connective of the linguistic and the behavioral needs to be emphasized so as to avoid a linguistic reductionism on the one hand and a behavioristic reductionism on the other hand. The hasty claims that all in the end boils down to how we use language or how we can quantify atomistic bits of behavior are claims that are not only one-sided but veritably occlude the vibrant texture of praxis as entwined discourse and action. What is required is a move to a *holistic* understanding and explanation of human thought and action.[25]

It is within the interstices of this amalgam of discourse and action, in the wake of the delimitation of ontology and the move into the ethical, that we discover the site of presence—not an abstract metaphysical presence but rather a concrete and pulsating embodied presence. In addressing the issue of presence, it is mandatory to return time and again to the phenomenon of embodiment—to the embodied self as present to itself in its encounter with the embodied other. The embodied other is present in the "face," and the face, as Levinas reminds us, is the principal manifestation of the more encompassing embodiment of the other: "The face is the expression of the Other (and the whole human body is in this sense more or less face)."[26] The other is present in his or her embodiment, in the outstretched arms of the beggar, in the mangled limbs of the cripple, in the pitiful cries of the orphan. Otherness is disclosed through the praxis of a perceptual decipherment of the bodily comportment of the other. The actional expression of praxis includes the moment of perception, and perception, as we have been taught by Maurice Merleau-Ponty, is made possible by the solicitations of embodiment across the figure-background horizon.

It is thus the field of praxis—and one does well to speak of praxis as a field instead of as serialized linguistic and behavioral episodes of behavior—is textured by an alterity, the otherness of the discourse and

---

25. For an extended discussion of the texture of praxis as an amalgam of discourse and action providing a backdrop for the twin moments of understanding and explanation, see Calvin O. Schrag, *Communicative Praxis and the Space of Subjectivity* (Bloomington: Indiana University Press, 1986), specifically chap. 4, "Understanding and Explanation as Ways of Interpretation," 72–93.

26. Emmanuel Levinas, *Ethics and Infinity*, trans. Richard A. Cohen (Pittsburgh: Duquesne University Press, 1985), 97.

action that solicits one's responses. Our discourse and action is always responsive to prior discourse and action. The self establishes its presence in its response to discourse and action that is always already extant. The presence of the self and the presence of the other become a shared presence. The unpacking of this notion of praxial presence, which is never an interior or self-enclosed presence but always conditioned by exteriority, needs to proceed along the lines of a dual comprehension of the effects of temporality and givenness. It is a presence situated between a past and a future, and it is a presence determined by its being presented, appearing on the scene as a given, thrust upon one, adventitious, coming from the outside as it were.

The salient point, on which much of what follows rests, is that the temporality and the givenness at issue require a delimitation of the range of objectification. As the present in our praxis-oriented lived history is not an "object," a reified instant of time, so the givenness of the discourse and action of the other escapes categorial objectivization. Since the seminal explorations of the texture of lived-time by Heidegger and Merleau-Ponty, it is no longer necessary to belabor the descriptions of the time of human existence in contradistinction to the metaphysical legacy of time as a measurement of serialized and objectified instants. The self that is present to itself in its insertion between a past and a future and the other that is present to the self in her preobjective givenness override the subject-object dichotomy of classical metaphysics and modern epistemology.

The phenomenon of alterity, insinuated into the heart of praxis, determining the existential givenness of discourse and action, language and social practices, provides the backdrop for what we have come to call the "ethic of the fitting response." Situated in the world in such a manner that the space of world experience is always invaded by prior discourse and action, the ethical requirement becomes that of discerning a response that is fitting for the occasion. It is important, however, that the fittingness at issue not be construed as a facile accommodation to the existing circumstances. Ethical discernment and judgment clearly require a consideration of extant moral directives and of the role that tradition plays in our social practices, but the fitting response is not simply beholden to any current moral state of affairs nor is it bound to the heritage of any given tradition. Indeed, that which is fitting may require a radical intervention and an abridgment of that to which a tradition has held fast. Herein resides our family quarrel with the ethical stance of those who place tradition in the forefront and see the narrative of our ethical life as basically shaped by the ingression of traditional norms and values.

The ethical approaches proposed by Alasdair MacIntyre and Hans-Georg Gadamer are cases in point. MacIntyre's "virtue ethics" is founded on the reclamation of a tradition, basically of an Aristotelian-Thomistic bent, that informs the directives for moral action. Why this particular tradition is selected to perform such an important function is never made all that clear. Nor is it all that evident that Aristotle and Saint Thomas Aquinas comprise such an unbroken solidarity of thought that would enable one to speak of a single tradition. Tradition is very much a *multiple* phenomenon. It needs properly to be spoken of in the plural. A similar problem comes to our attention as we peruse Gadamer's "hermeneutical ethic," in which tradition supplies the springs for moral behavior. What is a problem in both of these approaches is a failure to recognize the weight of the differences among competing traditions, the reality of tradition always in the plural, as well as the need to achieve the requisite distance from any given tradition in the exercise of internal and external critique.

An ethic of the fitting response, on the hither side of the bifurcation of theory and practice, is not to be mistaken for a new ethical theory. Nor does it provide supplementary theoretical grounding to reinforce one's teleological, deontological, or utilitarian conceptual schemes. The grounding of ethical theory in a doctrine of ends, or in a doctrine of duty, or in a doctrine of utility designed to achieve the maximal good for the greatest number, all needs to be suspended. Not only do we recommend a "teleological suspension of the ethical" à la Kierkegaard, but a deontological and a utilitarian suspension as well. And we recommend a suspension of these multiple ethical theories that have played such an important role in the philosophical history of Western ethical theory because the first question that needs to be asked is not, What is my distinctive end as a rational being? nor, What is my incontrovertible duty? nor, What is the greatest good for myself and my community? but rather, What is going on in the discourse and action that is thrust upon me in my concrete facticity? More specifically, the question achieves its existential intensification when the alterity of the discourse and action that impinges on my concrete facticity becomes manifest in asking about a who rather than a what. Reduced to its existential nudity, the ethical question becomes, Who stands before me and issues a summons with her voice and visage calling on me to respond? Acknowledging an alterity of a discourse and action that antedates the presence of myself to myself, I am called to assume the stance of responsibility and respond to that which is not of my own making.

This prioritizing of the question that guides the fitting response does not by any means reduce the significance of questions concerning ends, duties, rights, and goods both social and natural. These questions all return, but they return in a transversal relativity in which each is delimited by the other, precluding any absolutizing of a particular moral norm and attenuating the zeal for theoretical grounding. The questions, What is my end? What is my duty? What are my rights? What is good for society? are all quite legitimate questions, but they lose their relevance when asked in abstraction from the facticity of impinging forces of nature and cultural trends. They are questions that presuppose a set of conditions in what is going on in advance of any reflections on ends, duties, rights, and social values.

The feuds between liberals and communitarians are instructive in that they highlight the interplay and tension between individual rights and the welfare of the wider community, but when these ethical positions become sedimented into ethical theories based on metaphysical claims regarding individual and group substances, the concrete dialectic of self-with-society becomes occluded. We have much to learn from the longstanding disputes between proponents of natural law and the advocates for positive law, but in the moment each party in the dispute makes claims for absolute theoretical grounding, our ethical vision becomes jaundiced. In making the hard ethical decisions on feeding the hungry, both at home and abroad, the natural drives and appetites of the human body need to be taken into account. There are bodily needs, inscribed by nature, that ought to be met. But these drives, appetites, and needs cannot be dissociated from deliberations on individual rights and social obligations, from moral duties and ethical norms. Nature and culture are entwined in an ongoing state of affairs that invites each and all to respond.

Praxis as the texture of the fitting response within the constraints of nature and culture supplies the site for a new notion of presence that is able to account at once for a "responding center" and a "soliciting presentment," both of which, as we have already observed, are required to fulfill the ethical demand for responsibility. But the very concept of a center is not without its problematic metaphysical encrustations. And here we have something to learn from Derrida, who already in his early deconstructionist period was able to find a space for a center properly articulated. In his classic reply to Serge Doubrovsky on this particular matter, Derrida made his position quite clear: "First of all, I didn't say that there was no center, that we could get along without a center. I believe that the center is a function, not a being—a reality, but a function. And this function is absolutely indispensable."[27] Here we observe Derrida marking out a trajectory of deconstruction that clears the path of the

27. Richard Macksey and Eugenio Donato, *The Languages of Criticism and the Sciences of Man: The Structuralist Controversy* (Baltimore, Md.: Johns Hopkins University Press, 1970), 271.

refuse left by metaphysical speculations on the center without deleting the concept of the center from philosophical discourse. Admittedly, at this stage in Derrida's deconstructive project we are left with a rather thin notion of the center as a grammatological function. The vocabulary of function is always problematic because it trades on the classical schema of a substance-function relation or the modern schema of a structure-function relation, prompting one to ask, a function of what? And the what, even on Derrida's own grammatological account, remains indeterminate for want of a trustworthy signifier.

In the later Derrida, however, the notion of a centered subject is filled out with ethical content, as is evident in his reply to Jean-Luc Nancy's query, "Who comes after the subject?" Derrida's reply is quick and straightforward. That which continues to be required by the question, Who? against the backdrop of both classical and later nonclassical definitions of the subject, is "a certain responsibility."[28] We thus see that there is life for the centered subject after deconstruction, albeit no longer that of a subject understood as a stable entity and no longer a center construed as a metaphysically anchored permanent present. What is called to our attention in the aftermath of the deconstruction of metaphysical entities and properties is the space of praxis—a space in which the subject undergoes a transfiguration into the who of discourse and action and the center comes into play as the site from which responsible thought and practice issue.

As the move to praxis provides us with the site for the responding center from which all fitting responses proceed, so also it sets the stage for an acknowledgment of the alterity of the soliciting presentment, which always antedates the deliberation and action that motivates the responding center and which provides an opening to the presence of the Deity in human affairs. And it is here we have much to learn from Levinas, specifically from his accentuation of the disclosure of the Deity in the face and call of the neighbor and the stranger, the afflicted and the suffering, in which there is a beckoning to a responsibility that points beyond the multiple responsibilities in the economy of civil society. It is this responsibility Levinas calls to our attention, somewhat hyperbolically, when he speaks of a responsibility beyond responsibility, an *impossible* responsibility, in which God "comes to mind"—or as we would be inclined to say, when God comes to presence.

The acknowledgment of a soliciting presence, particularly in its intensification of pushing the human subject to its limits, facilitates both an understanding of the emphasis in the prophetic message on heeding

28. Cadava, Connor, and Nancy, eds., *Who Comes after the Subject?* 100.

the call of God and doing his will and the truth of the sacramental principle attesting to the presence of the sacred in the secular. The ethical presence of praxis, at the heart of the prophetic message, points to a presence beyond the presence of the other self in her discourse and action, a presence beyond the economy of intersubjectivity, an aneconomic presence on the fringes of the horizon of the intramundane lifeworld. So also the presence attested to in ritual performances and in the celebration of the sacraments is a presence embodied in natural kinds and in artifacts. The water in the baptismal ritual, the wine and the bread in the Eucharist, the assorted icons of both Eastern and Western religion, testify to a creative and regenerative power in the world of nature. All this demands a reconsideration of the objectivized view of nature that is so much a legacy of the Enlightenment. The facile separation of nature and history, the physical world and the cultural world, needs to be brought into question.

Here again, Merleau-Ponty's penetrating analysis of embodiment, in which the body as lived is at once nature and culture, at once experiencing and being experienced, provides an avenue for overcoming an unacceptable dichotomy and dualism that has been with us all too long. As one moves out from the experience of one's own body as a way of existing in the world, as a task to be done, as the place from which one's projects emanate, to the presence of the embodiment of the other self through whom I understand my own embodiment, and then to the more encompassing phenomenon of institutional embodiment, we begin to understand the site in which sacramental and ritual presence begin to take on a form and function that avoids the snares of idolatry. Whether one is dealing with the presence of the spirit of Buddha in the display of his likeness or the presence of the embodiment of the mission of Christ in the elements of the bread and the wine, we are dealing with a presence that overflows the restricted economy of physical and chemical elements and properties. The iconic forms and elements at issue here testify of the infinite compassion of the Buddha and the infinite love manifest in the narrative of the Christ, symbolized in the institution of the church as the "*body* of Christ." This provides a sheet anchor against the claims for a nonsymbolic standing-in-itself presence of a deity in a transubstantiated or consubstantiated element of nature and artifact of culture. A sustained vigilance over the incursions of a sacramental literalism is required to forestall the facile slippage of an icon into an idol.

Our effort to achieve some understanding of the meaning of ethical and sacramental presence within the praxial economy of nature and history has led us to focus on that which impinges on this economy, breaks into it from an exterior, an alterity that is other than the otherness of mundane transcendence. This is an alterity that announces its presence in the guise of an impossible responsibility, impossible within an economy that bears the mark of Cain, the human all-too-human. It is the responsibility of responding with infinite compassion and infinite love, and this is a love, as Levinas has observed, that is not the love of eros, not the conditional love that expects something in return, but rather a love that requires no repayment, a love outside the economy of distribution and exchange. In making this move to the vocabulary of infinite compassion and infinite love, one may well be best served by a new semantics of the gift.

In proceeding to a semantics of the gift, we are projecting a move beyond the ethical as such. The trajectory that we are pursuing follows the line from a delimitation of metaphysics and ontology en route to the ethical to a delimitation of the ethical itself. The truth of the ethical as the fitting response culminates in the truth of the religious within the acknowledgment and response to the gift. That there is a family resemblance in this trajectory to Kierkegaard's well-known "stages on life's way," whereby one proceeds from the aesthetical to the ethical and then to the religious, is of course undeniable. We are, however, concerned to avoid the all too common misreading of Kierkegaard's doctrine of the stages— more properly dubbed existence-spheres—as independent forms of life, radically isolated from each other, serially juxtaposed in such a manner that when one moves to the other, the previous stage is simply left behind. In the end, the aesthetical, the ethical, and the religious, according to Kierkegaard, are to be properly viewed as intercalating and interdependent modes or ways of existing in the world. But this does not obliterate important distinctions between the three stages or existence-spheres. The distinctions between the aesthetical, the ethical, and the religious are indeed distinctions that make a difference. Hence, it is important to recognize that in the move to the religious, although both the aesthetical and the ethical are revisited, they are nonetheless transfigured from self-contained resources for living into modes of life beholden to the call of an alterity that issues from a region beyond the aesthetical and ethical economies themselves.

It is thus that Kierkegaard has much to teach us about the errors of aestheticism and moralism alike. The history of aestheticism extends far back into ancient times, receiving intermittent expression in claims for art as a panacea for all of humanity's ills. The "new" aestheticism of postmodernism is but an avatar of the old. Nietzsche needs to be held at least partly responsible for this new idolatry of the aesthetical consciousness. He certainly provided an invitation to the absolutization of the aesthetical in his preachments that we have art so as not to die of truth and that it is only in the aesthetic phenomenon that life achieves its justification. For this reason his projected master morality, modeled after an aesthetic ideal, remains unable to muster the requisite resources to slay the dragons of nihilism. Aesthetically based master morality issues a call for the affirmation of life as life, but affirmation in the name of what or whom? Apparently in the name of the principle of all principles, namely the will-to-power. But as we have already observed, the relation of power to the achievement of justice in civil society remains undetermined in the Nietzschean corpus, and power untempered by justice remains vulnerable to the insidious forces of self and societal destruction.

It is not as though Nietzsche lacked all opportunities for securing a religious content in his moral imperative to affirm life. His reactive atheism was not of the pedestrian sort that simply negates the concept of God in classical theistic metaphysics. This concept of God for Nietzsche is indeed "dead," but there are intimations of a God beyond the God spoken of in theism and atheism alike. Here again we return to the theme of power—more precisely the theme of the Will-to-Power in bold-face capitals. But power without love is as ineffectual as is power without justice in providing the necessary conditions for meeting the challenges along life's way. Here too, however, Nietzsche had the opportunity for integrating power, love, and justice in his suggestive notion of the "gifting virtue," but this is one of the many suggestive notions in Nietzsche's thought that remained undeveloped. And it remained undeveloped principally because Nietzsche was unable to dislodge gift giving from a virtue-based ethic. As otherwise than being, the gift surpasses any enumeration and ranking of virtues.

An even more pronounced gesture toward an aestheticism that short-circuits both the ethical and the religious moments can be found in the writings of Foucault, even though an effort is made by Foucault to carve out a space for what he has termed an "ethic of care" in his later writings. His earlier focus was an analysis of social practices in which he gave detailed descriptions of the entwinement of power relations that lead to a virtual subjugation of the subject. His principal interest, however, he informs us, has always been in developing a hermeneutics of the subject that would make explicit the dynamics of a more positive process of self-formation, illustrating an ethic of care as a "practice of freedom."[29]

This ethic of care, we soon discover, is to be aesthetically grounded. The paradigm of such an aesthetically based ethic, according to Fou-

29. See Michel Foucault, "The Ethic of Care for the Self as a Practice of Freedom," in *The Final Foucault*, ed. James Bernauer and David Rasmussen (Cambridge, Mass.: MIT Press, 1988).

cault, can be found in Stoicism, which he understands as having been antinormative from bottom up, its principal aim defined as aesthetic in character, devised for a small elite who were interested solely in personal choices that motivate the living of an aesthetically harmonious life: "I don't think we can find any normalization in, for instance, the Stoic ethics. The reason is, I think, that the principal aim, the principal target of this kind of ethics was an aesthetic one. First, this kind of ethics was only a problem of personal choice. Second, it was reserved for a few people in the population; it was not a question of giving a pattern of behavior for everybody. It was a personal choice for a small elite. The reason for making this choice was the *will* to live a beautiful life."[30]

It thus becomes evident that the age-old problem of the relation of the ethical to the aesthetical, and the reemergence of the specter of aestheticism, is a problem that does not seem to go away. Kierkegaard grasped this problem with an unparalleled profundity and taught that a resolution of the problem cannot proceed without attention to the role and function of the religious. Hence, from time to time it will be necessary to solicit help from Kierkegaard in our own journey along the stages of life's way as we proceed to the final chapter and probe the region beyond the economies of the aesthetical and the ethical, which in the most general of all terms we will name the region of an entwined *topos* and *utopos* of the gift.

30. James Miller, *The Passion of Michel Foucault* (New York: Simon and Schuster, 1993), 346.

4

From Ethics to the Gift

The Gift and Transcendence

The delimitation of ontology provides an occasion to reformulate the question about ethics in such a manner so as to be given priority over the question about being. Before being, the ethical is announced as the call to responsibility. We have named this call to responsibility an invocation to perform a fitting response. In tracking the move from the ontological to the ethical we have found Plato and Levinas to be trustworthy mentors. We have heeded Plato's counsel that the Good is indeed *epekeina tes ousias,* exceeding the structures of being in dignity and power, and we have given credence to Levinas's instruction on the alterity of the face and the call of the other as veritably otherwise than being.

However, in proceeding to an inquiry into a semantics of the gift, we are carrying through another delimitation—this time a delimitation of the ethical itself. From one perspective this can be understood as a radicalization of Plato's and Levinas's delimitation of the being question; from another perspective it can be seen as at once a transvaluation of Plato's ultimate principle and Levinas's ethic of responsibility. The Good in the thought of Plato and the ethical as conceived by Levinas are indeed otherwise than being. But the gift is older than either the Good or the ethical, surpassing both as a resource for our discourse and action. The task is to free the gift from both Being and the Good. The gift is not only anterior to the ontic determinations of the totality of beings and the ontological disclosure of the Being of beings; it also antedates the asking of the question about the ethical.

Nietzsche understood clearly enough the need to proceed beyond the traditional value categories associated with the sedimented distinctions between good and evil. The message of Zarathustra is quite clear on this point. The traditional value categories have conspired to produce a herd morality—a morality for the weak in spirit, a morality that levels everyone to a common denominator, a morality bereft of creativity, leading to an evisceration of life itself. Hence, Nietzsche saw fit to propose a transvaluation of all hitherto existing values in the interests of establishing a master morality to counter the stultifying precepts that guide the herd. But Nietzsche's project fell short of the mark, unable to dispel the specter of European nihilism, and in the end succumbed to a species of aestheticism. The will to power, the lynchpin of master morality, was destined to take an aesthetic turn. Style takes precedence over ethical content as we are advised to look to the arts for redemption. Nietzsche may indeed have been correct in his diagnosis of the ills of Western culture, but he came up short in his prescription for a cure. His intermittent intimations of a transvalued virtue of gift giving and gift receiving remained undeveloped and kept him at a distance from the truth of the gift as the proper content for a viable morality.

Nietzsche remained unable to free the gift from the economy of exchange relations that transform the gift into an expectation that solicits a return. This return may be nothing more than an expression of gratitude, a responding thank-you. The receiver of the gift thanks the giver. But in the thanking of someone for a gift, there is the acknowledgment that a form of service has been graciously rendered, and the implication is that the recipient was weak and needed help. In performing a service in giving a gift, the giver does for the recipient what the recipient could not do for herself or himself. The recipient of a gift is someone who needs help and hence is degraded in the minds of both the giver and the recipient. But then the recipient thanks the giver for the gift and in doing so degrades the giver as someone who has to serve the needs of the recipient. In thanking the giver, the recipient elevates herself or himself to the status of mastery and degrades the giver of the gift to the status of servitude. Reduced to the status of filling a need, the gift functions as a coefficient of bondage within a matrix of exchange relations. This, according to Nietzsche, is the vicious cycle of gift exchange, illustrative, quite clearly, of Hegel's celebrated master/servant dialectic.

In turning our attention to narratives about the gift, we will take up intermittent conversations with those who have already offered different perspectives on what is at issue in the giving and receiving of gifts. In doing so, we intend to advance our investigations into a new semantics for talking about God. In the previous chapter we pondered over the coming to presence of the Deity in the prophetic voice and in the sacramental ritual, and we became perplexed about the meaning and status of presence in these longstanding expressions of the religious consciousness. The word and the will of God are alleged to present themselves in the ethical requirement of responsibility and the sacred is attested to as present in the sacraments. But in what manner is the dimension of the holy and the sacred present in these prophetic/ethical and priestly/sacramental practices? What soliciting presentment is in operation here, and what is the texture of the space and the time of presence that enables one to receive the soliciting presentment? We have already observed that there is much ado about presence in these matters, and we have suggested that one need keep the question about presence in proximity to the question about praxis.

As we move to narratives on the gift, we find that the notion of presence is also very much at issue. Gifts are presented, apparently by someone to someone. It is common to speak of gifts as presents. When we give a gift, we give a present; when we receive a gift, we receive a present. A gift to be a gift needs to be presented, which means among other things that it needs to be given away. And it needs to be given away freely, without compulsion. The practice of gift giving also requires that the gift be accepted, this likewise without compulsion. But what is at work in the receiving of a gift? It is commonly believed that gifts should be acknowledged. Their presence should be noted in some manner or other, if by nothing more than a simple thank-you. But here we seem to gravitate into an unexpected aporia. How can one acknowledge a gift without reducing it to a debt that requires some species of repayment? Does not the gift, to be truly a gift, require the total absence of signals and signs for a return of something in kind? Does not a gift need to be exempt from presence, external to that which can be presented, leading to the rather odd conceptual predicament that a gift can never be a present.

Reflections on gift giving and gift receiving can be found in various philosophical and theological texts from the Greeks onward. It was, however, the highly acclaimed text by Marcel Mauss, *Essai sur le don, forme archaique de l'Echange,* published in 1924, that brought the topic of the gift into prominence.[1] In this work Mauss analyzes and describes the practices of gift giving and gift receiving in primitive societies, in which he found these practices to play a not inconsequential role. Although distinguished from the exchange of goods and services as this exchange is defined in advanced market-modeled societies, gifts in the primitive societies Mauss studied were nonetheless viewed in conjunction with loosely defined principles of distribution and exchange.

Gift giving was accepted as a practice that had its own obligatory restraints. Members of the various tribes were obligated to give and re-

---

1. The English translation of Mauss's essay was first published in Great Britain in 1990 by Routledge and was later reissued as a Norton paperback. See *The Gift: The Form and Reason for Exchange in Archaic Societies,* trans. W. D. Halls (London: W. W. Norton, 1990).

ceive gifts, and they were obligated to repay in some fashion the giver of gifts. The practice thus took on the coloring of gift *exchange*. Gifts were defined against the backdrop of an economy of exchange relations. Hence, gifts were not distributed in a disinterested manner. They were in fact viewed as means to gain honor or status within their respective tribes and in many instances simply became instruments of commerce among the different tribes. The gift, as explained by Mauss, performed the function of maintaining human solidarity in archaic societies.

Gift exchange had a leavening effect on the quality of life among the various tribes, supplying not only an economic but also a moral catalyst. It is thus that Mauss characterizes gift exchanges as "*total* social facts," understood as phenomena that "are at the same time juridical, economic, religious, and even aesthetical and morphological."[2] This leavening ingredient, however, with its moral and religious features was not understood as an abridgment of the inchoate forces of production and consumption, distribution and exchange, that informed even primitive societies. Yet, the lesson to be learned from the practice of giving gifts in these early forms of social organization is that gift exchange can provide a measure of moderation to the inequities of the accumulation of wealth in increasingly technologized market economies.

It was Jacques Derrida who in *Given Time* radicalized Mauss's economics of the gift and problematized the very concept of gift exchange. Derrida's principal point is that the insertion of gift giving into a network of exchange relations results in a virtual negation of the gift as a gift. Within any economy of exchange relations, a gift inevitably incurs indebtedness, even if only in the guise of the customary practice of thanking someone for a gift. In thanking someone for a gift we are acknowledging a deed that has been done for us, and in this acknowledgment we are already giving something back. A genuine gift, in its purity of being freely given without any expectation of return, would need to be forgotten in the very moment that it is given and received. It cannot be acknowledged as a gift by either party. But this all congeals into an aporia of gift giving and gift receiving as an impossibility. In the moment a gift is given, it succumbs to an interplay of exchange relations. Strictly speaking, a gift can neither be given nor can it be received. Such is the account *given* by Derrida, placing us in a bit of a quandary as to how one might *accept* the account!

What is required, surely, is an effort to achieve maximal clarity on the issue at hand. This will demand some studied attention to the peculiar

2. Ibid., 79.

conditions that give rise to the alleged aporia of giving and receiving gifts as an impossibility. The conditions that inform the aporia have to do principally with the semantic interplay of possession and dispossession, reserve and expenditure, surplus and squandering, having and giving. It is these conditions, among others to be sure, that set the stage for the catapulting of the gift into an economy of exchange relations. It would appear the very conditions that create the aporia in the giving and receiving of gifts reside within a matrix of social relations based on the accumulation of wealth and the institution of private ownership. If giving a gift is dispossessing oneself of something that one has previously owned, then it clearly is the case that private ownership supplies the very conditions for the distribution and exchange of gifts. To be able to dispossess oneself of something presupposes prior possession or ownership. One cannot dispossess without first possessing. Gift giving would then find its foundation in an economy of production and exchange relations in which only those who are privileged by ownership of private property are truly able to give. Objects need first to be produced, distributed, and owned before they can be given away. Such is the position taken by Michael Walzer, who has supplied what may be a not uncommon view on the practice of gift giving. "If I can shape my identity through my possessions," he writes, "then I can do so through my dispossessions. And, even more surely, what I can't possess, I can't give away."[3]

Entwined with this consumerist definition of gift giving as gift exchange there are, of course, a host of presuppositions regarding the extension of the metaphor of possession not only to the human subject's relation to the goods of the earth but veritably to the human subject itself. To analyze the gift back into a framework of possession and dispossession, reserve and expenditure, is at once to privilege the private over the public and fail to discern that objects given as gifts never issue from a zero-point origin of absolute ownership. The meaning of ownership itself, particularly as it relates to the social practice of gift giving, requires inspection. From a less consumerist perspective, the grammar of custodian and steward might be more fitting than that of owner in characterizing one's relation to nature. The goods of the earth and the services of humankind can indeed become privatized, but such privatization needs to recognize the subordination of personal ownership and property rights to an acknowledgment of the earth as an abode shared by all of its inhabitants. Rather than the earth belonging to us, parceled

3. Michael Walzer, *Spheres of Justice: A Defense of Pluralism and Equality* (New York: Basic Books, 1983), 123.

out as our property, it might advance an understanding of our relation to the earth by viewing it as that to which we belong. To give a gift is to acknowledge the facticity of preexistent natural kinds, antedating their distribution in artificially constructed private and public spheres. In addition, the claim by Walzer that one shapes one's identity through one's possessions and dispossessions belies a rather thin notion of self-identity indeed. Those unfortunate ones without possessions are destined to exist without knowledge of who they are!

It is thus the consumerist perspective on the gift invites a consumerist theory of self-identity and a consumerist morality. The metaphor of possession is extended in such a manner that it encompasses the accumulation of moral properties. The moral self is portrayed as a storehouse of virtues, a surplus of moral acquisitions, which the self is obligated to give away in fulfilling its moral duties to others. Morality takes on its determinations against the backdrop of an ethical economy of virtues, duties, and rights that assume meaning only in terms of reciprocal exchange values. Gift giving as a virtue, what Nietzsche named "*die schenkende Tugend*," can quickly degenerate into a practice that in the end wants to be paid well. The gift needs to be returned in some fashion. If gift giving is the performance of a virtuous act, reaching a crowning fulfillment in self-sacrifice, the giving of oneself for the welfare of another, one needs to be in possession of a moral attribute or quality that one now freely gives to the other.

The moral task, within this presuppositional framework, becomes that of storing up an excess of moral traits, fleshing out a kind of moral curriculum vitae, defining one's identity through a possession of surplus virtue, then perfecting the moral life through a dispossession of that which one has in superabundance. The moral life in civil society then becomes as much a victim of consumerism as does one's socioeconomic existence. The consequent challenge to be met is that of liberating the gift, the giving and receiving of gifts, from the restricted economies that govern our social and ethical life. Meeting this challenge will require that we give particular attention to the dynamics of the gift as an event in our discourse and action that draws its measure from a source other than the economies informed by production and consumption, distribution, and exchange. A genuine gift will need to issue from an aneconomic region. The dynamics of the gift comes into view only in the wake of the suspension of the "law (*nomos*) of the *oikos*," understood as the rules, regulations, and requirements that govern the organization of the family, the household, the mundanity of the familiar and quotidian practices of everyday life. The gift transgresses law.

To acknowledge the gift as gift, both in its being given and in its being received, is to attest to an alterity that transcends the categories of ownership and excess, accumulation and surplus, possession and dispossession, as they insinuate our moral life. As one observes the slide from the uses of the categories of production and exchange in the narrowly restricted economy of the world of commerce to the moral categories of recompense and remuneration, reward and retribution, that play in the laws of our ethical economies, it is of particular moment to attest to the gift as otherwise than being and on the hither side of the standardized categories of good and evil. The gift is a testimony to a radical transcendence of both the civic and the moral order. That which is presented as a gift needs to be presented without an expectation of return—without any anticipation of a repayment in kind or by something of equal value. Indeed, the very notions of counter-gift and gift exchange are conceptually incoherent. A gift, genuinely given, can neither be countered nor become an item to which one ascribes an exchange value. Such would reduce the gift to an implied contractual agreement. In effect, it would annul the very conditions for genuine gift giving. The gift event requires that the recipient be freed from an obligation to reciprocate, lest the receiving of the gift be debased as an incursion of a debt that requires repayment.

The central point that needs to be underscored and reemphasized is that the gift is outside of, external to, independent of, and in a quite robust sense otherwise than the economy of interactions within our personal and social existence. It is radically transcendent to the requirements for reciprocity and balanced ledgers of exchange that are legislated by the laws of the *oikos*. Thus understood, the gift does indeed appear to be very much the impossibility that Derrida judges it to be. Yet, the peculiar texture, status, and meaning of this impossibility calls for further clarification. One needs to move from general explications of the gift as gift to a particular exemplification or illustration of what might count as an impossibility of gift giving. Such a move was already suggested in the discussion of the perplexities that attach to the notion of presence in the prophetic and priestly functions of religion.

Both the prophet and the priest speak of a presence of the holy and the sacred. Marion, as noted, suggests that we think of the presence of the sacred in the Eucharist not as an esoteric chemical transformation but rather as the attestation of charity. Marion's summary definition of the eucharistic presence is that which is "deduced from the commitment of charity." As also noted, Levinas, a voice from another religious tradition, a spokesperson for a reclamation of the prophetic call of conscience, proclaims that the presence of the "God who comes to mind" needs to be understood in terms of a love that is not to be confused with eros. And both Marion's overture to charity as the founding reality of the sacraments and Levinas's ethic of responsibility tempered by love are reinforced by an earlier discourse on the subject—that of Kierkegaard's quite unparalleled *Works of Love.*

We thus find in the workings of love a singular exemplification of the gift. It is here we have a phenomenon in the form of a practice that expects nothing in return, a practice that is motivated by the sheer resources of its potential. Freely given, and given time and again, love is a performing and effecting that is done without intent of remuneration or anticipation of recompense. Plainly enough, the love at issue is a distinct kind of love, not to be confused with either *eros* or *philia*, as Levinas has cautioned. This is a love that does not expect anything to be given back. No laws or rules of reward and retribution enter into the dynamics of its eventing. As a superlative exemplification of the gift, beyond the economy of commensurate returns, otherwise than being, surpassing our conventional construals of good and evil, this unconditional love was already announced in the Greek and Latin vocabularies of *agapē* and *caritas.*

With the instantiation of the gift as love, external to the economies of distribution and exchange, reward and recompense, we have an occasion to refigure and revise the metaphysical concept of transcendence, which has been such a bane for classical theism. Making purchases on the concept of God as in some modality of being a supernatural entity external to finite time and space, it was not unexpected that theists would soon begin to talk of God as infinite in some metaphysical sense. To speak of God as metaphysically infinite is to define his mode of being as very different in substance and attributes from, and at best analogous to, the substance and attributes that comprise finite entities. The relation between such an infinite being and the world as a manifold of finite beings quickly became construed as a relation of causality and dependence. God as infinite being is the cause of the finite world. And as the concept of God in classical theism was informed by a metaphysics of substance, so also was this the case with the theists' concept of the world as a cosmos of finite inert and living substances, from the smallest quanta of matter to the highest levels of the human mind.

The deconstruction of the tenets of classical metaphysics of theism, detailed in part 1 of this study, has shifted attention away from the concept of *theos* that fueled the recurring debates between theists and atheists. This opens a new perspective for talking about God, problematizing the concept of transcendence in classical theism, a concept that was based on the metaphysical determination of the infinite as the culminating point in the scale of being. In the shift from a metaphysical grammar to a semantics of the gift, we have landed on the notion of the gift as transcendent, otherwise than being, beyond the infinite and the finite as metaphysical schema. This transcendence of the gift, in its concrete expression of a love devoid of any expectation of repayment, is an aneconomic transcendence. It is otherwise than the *nomos,* both implicit and explicit, that governs the commerce of human interactions, which remain beholden to the authorities and established mores of civil society. Insofar as the gift exceeds even the domain of the ethical, the transcendence at issue cannot be construed as a moment within the ethical itself—a move that was made in certain expressions of nineteenth- and early-twentieth-century liberal theology, which sought to reduce religion to morality.

Liberal theology, in spite of its trenchant critique of the tradition, continued to invest in the metaphysical depictions of the infinite and the finite as they pertain to the nature of God and his relation to the world. Displeased with the putatively unbridgeable gulf between an infinite deity and a finite world, theological liberals devised their own end run around the problem and sought to locate the metaphysical infinite in the finite. Much of the philosophical inspiration for doing so came from Hegel and his later philosophy of identity, which culminated in a mediation of the infinite and the finite. According to Hegel, this mediation was adumbrated by the religious consciousness of Christianity with its symbol of the Incarnation. But the intimations of the religious consciousness for Hegel (as well as those of the aesthetic consciousness) only achieve the realization of their potential when they are philosophically comprehended within the dialectics of the Absolute Idea. And it is this comprehension of what stands in for ultimate reality in Hegel's system that instructs us on the identity of the infinite and the finite, opening up a vision of God within the depths of the self as fully realized consciousness. A philosophy of identity, grounded on the primacy of consciousness, is able to solve the classical metaphysical problem of the relation of an infinite deity to a finite world by taking the doctrine of the Incarnation with utmost seriousness and construing it as the eternal presence of the infinite in the finite. God's status is no longer a mystery. The Deity resides within the interior depths of the finite soul.

It was principally against Hegel's doctrines of mediation and identity that Kierkegaard launched his impassioned existential revolt. To mediate the infinite and the finite is to dissolve the reality of both. An infinite God who is found in the depths of the finite soul is no longer God, and the self that seeks to constitute itself as infinite loses itself as finite self. On the contemporary scene Levinas occasioned a similar confrontation with Hegel's philosophy of identity, and in this respect Levinas would seem to be very much of one mind with Kierkegaard and his existential protest. Holding out for an accentuated sense of the transcendence of God, which he finds hinted at in the intriguing passage in *Meditations* where Descartes gives primacy to the notion of the infinite over the finite, Levinas is in accord with Kierkegaard that God is indeed wholly other, related to the finite only under the conditions of an asymmetry which no Hegelian dialectic of reciprocity is able to penetrate.

The problem that the contrasting positions of Hegel and Levinas bring to the fore is at once old and new. The relation between an infinite God and a finite world is a problem that has a long-standing tradition. Very much at the core of this problem is the meaning of transcendence. In the one case, transcendence is a qualification of consciousness within the interior depths of subjectivity. In the other case, transcendence is a determination of "absolute exteriority." In both cases, we find an attendant eschatology. The eschatology of Hegel is a *realized* eschatology, informed by a philosophy of identity, in which the Kingdom of God has already come to its fulfillment in the "eternal now" of our historical becoming. The eschatology of Levinas draws its inspiration from a philosophy of difference, in which the Kingdom of God is always deferred, yet to come, to unfold in the fullness of time that is never that of a present.

The move to a semantics of the gift requires that we readdress this age-old problem, albeit no longer as a metaphysical problem. The gift, we have seen, is indeed transcendent. Yet, supposedly gifts are given in the transactions of our social existence. Love as the quintessential exemplification of the gift, in the form of a *caritas,* a charity that is unconditional, expecting nothing in return, not even the repayment of loving the one who loves, remains an impossible venture given the human-all-too-human proclivities of our being in the world. Nonetheless, one is commanded to love one's neighbor as oneself, and at times one is motivated to do so. But how can this transcendent gift of love became efficacious within the immanental economies that are based on moral reciprocity, distributive justice, and political equality?

The Gift as Logos and Kairos

The gift is transcendent. Indeed it is transcendence *par excellence,* hyperbolic in its unconditionality. It is conditioned neither by a lack within its own resources nor by a telos of expectation of commensurate return. Yet, the gift has become part of our discourse and our action. We speak of gift giving and gift receiving, and we continue to give and receive gifts in spite of the apparent impossibility of doing so. Transcending the laws of exchange in the economy of human affairs, we nonetheless testify of the presence of gifts within the time and space of our communicative practices.

How is such to be comprehended? What is the peculiar "logic" of the gift whereby it can be both wholly transcendent to and yet immanent within the economies of our quotidian workaday world? Levinas forces us to ask this question when he testifies that the infinite face of God "comes to mind" in the finite face of the neighbor. Wherein resides the trace of the infinite in the finite? Kierkegaard compels us to address the very same issue when he has us reflect on the riddle of living in eternity while hearing the hall clock strike. What logic governs the incarnation of the gift, infinite and eternal in the sense proposed by Levinas and Kierkegaard, within "the political economy of civil society and human rights"?[4] Derrida raises this question in a peculiarly poignant manner when he alludes to the "movement of the gift that renounces itself, hence a movement of infinite love." But this infinite love is destined to become finite. "Only infinite love can renounce itself," continues Derrida, "and, in order to *become finite*, become incarnated in order to love the other, to love the other as a finite other."[5] But how can such be? What logic governs the incarnation of an infinite gift within the assorted economies of human finitude?

Might it be that to ask about the logic of the gift is singularly inappropriate, if not indeed scandalous? In speaking of a logic of gift giving and gift receiving is there not a danger of catapulting us back into an economy of exchange, founded on a *nomos,* a system of laws and criteria for quantification that governs the distribution of signifiers within a predicate calculus? And would this not enframe the gift within the strictures of a logic of identity and an epistemology of representation in which the signifiers and the signifieds pertaining to the gift would remain forever undecidable? If one is to speak of a logic of the gift it will need to be understood as that of a quite special sort, possibly akin to the "logic of practice" in Pierre Bourdieu's influential book by that name, in which he makes much of the fact that gift giving does not follow the social rules

4. The phrase is the descriptive title of Gary B. Madison's comprehensive study of the interdependent spheres of the moral, the cultural, and the political as they inform the economy of our sociohistorical existence. See Madison, *The Political Economy of Civil Society and Human Rights* (New York: Routledge, 1998).

5. Jacques Derrida, *The Gift of Death,* trans. David Wills (Chicago: University of Chicago Press, 1995), 51.

of commodity exchange; or one might explicate the logic in question as taking its cues from Alan Schrift's edited volume, *The Logic of the Gift*, in which it becomes readily evident that the logic that has to do with the gift cannot be that which issues from a technocratic conception of rationality.[6]

It may be helpful at this juncture to recall the history of logic and its early associations with the time-honored concept of the logos. Although the objectification and quantification the exercise of logic requires suspends the infusion of the historical, logic too has its history as a disciplinary matrix. As the specialized science of valid and invalid reasoning, it had its origins in the Greek concept of the logos as a unifying principle of rationality. It was in this grand hypothesis of an ontologically based rationality that the technical/methodological rationality of logic had its source. Without disparaging the role and function of logic as a highly specialized discipline, clearly possessing its own integrity and legitimacy, it may be less misleading to speak of the logos of the gift rather than the logic of the gift.

The grammar of the logos, however, both in its ancient and its modern expression, has come under critical scrutiny in various postmodern enclaves. We are cautioned time and again about the incursions of a logocentrism with its undeliverable claims for universality, necessity, and identity. Plainly enough, the gift cannot be a logocentric principle, neither in its ancient ontological nor in its modern epistemological dress. Yet, if the gift as transcendent and aneconomic is to play a role in the economy of our communicative practices and its amalgamated discourse and action, then it will need to display a structure of meaning so as to make an apprehension of it possible. The gift, although otherwise than being, transcendent and wholly other, suffers disclosure in the time and space of human transactions.

The message of this disclosure of the gift as logos in the rough and tumble of human events is not a message of particularly recent date. John the Evangelist, in the Prologue to his Gospel, already announced that the logos was not only with God from time immemorial but that it indeed *was* God, and that the logos became flesh and dwelt among us. It then became the mission of Saint John in his first Epistle to provide the climax in the plot of the Evangelist's narrative about the logos. The logos that

6. Pierre Bourdieu, *The Logic of Practice*, trans. Richard Nice (Cambridge, England: Polity Press, 1990); and Alan D. Schrift, ed., *The Logic of the Gift: Toward an Ethic of Generosity* (New York: Routledge, 1997).

has become flesh is love. "God is love (*agapē*)" is Saint John's consummate statement on the matter (I John 4:8).

In the history of Christian doctrine, the Evangelist's spin on the logos came to be called the "logos doctrine" of Johannine Christology. Christ is the logos, present with God from the very beginning, defined by the church fathers at the First Council of Nicea (A.D. 325) as veritably of the same substance (*homoousion*) as that of God. Insofar as the logos came to be understood as fully present in the person of Christ, incarnate in the body of the Jesus of Nazareth, it was incumbent upon the church fathers to take up the issue of the "two natures" in the person of Jesus Christ. This all came to a head at the Council of Chalcedon (A.D. 451), where disputing parties sorted out the often conflicting views on the person and nature of Jesus Christ and decided that the least misleading creedal formula should read that in the incarnated event there is "one person" but "two natures," one divine and one human, inseparable but not to be confused, highlighting the peculiarity of each nature concurrent in one person.

Much of what happened at the historic Councils of Nicea and Chalcedon would seem to have its source in the doctrine of the logos as set forth in the Gospel according to John. Greek grammar provides the matrix for the formulation of both the Trinitarian and the Christological doctrines of the early church. It is thus that John the Evangelist can be properly dubbed as the "most Greek" of the four Gospel writers. Yet, one must keep in mind that the concept of the logos is not the restricted property of Greek thought, on loan to the church fathers to aid them in formulating their theological creeds as they define the peculiar task of a logos of theos. The concept of the logos, albeit of a somewhat different stripe, can also be found in the writings of the "wisdom literature" of the ancient Hebrews.

What is of particular moment for us in our narrative is that in the doctrinal development of both Christianity and Judaism, the vocabulary of Greek philosophy came to play an increasingly important role. Both Christian and Jewish medieval theologians adapted the Greek concept of the logos to their own purposes, and in each case the logos took on the lineaments of substantiality, causal efficacy, supreme perfection, universality in its omnipotence and omniscience—all composing a rather bold metaphysical inventory. Such was the destiny of theistic metaphysics in Western thought. This was the fate of the logos in the service of theology. What the testimony of the logos as *love* might have to do with these formal and abstract designators is something surely not all that clear on the face of it. It would appear the metaphysical conceptions of God and the Incarnation do not shake out particularly well for advancing the attestation of an unconditional love that has no telos for repayment.

The fate of the logos doctrine of the ancient Hebrews and of the early Christian community as it became ensnared in the clutches of a grand metaphysical narrative found its counterpart in a developing epistemology that pretty much traveled side by side with classical and modern metaphysics. If the distinctions between the infinite and the finite, the eternal and the temporal, are construed along the lines of a metaphysical divide, defining the infinite and eternal as a being of a superlative sort to be distinguished from the realm of finite and temporal beings—as was clearly the case in classical theistic metaphysics—then any talk of the presence of the former in the latter will tax the resources of human reason. Against the backdrop of such a schema of opposition, any testimony of an incarnation—whether of a Jewish, Christian, or Islamic sort—will indeed result in a crucifixion of the understanding. For Greek logocentrism, any such claims remain scandalous, as they do also for a theistic metaphysics that keeps the metaphysical signifiers intact. Within the folds of such a metaphysical divide, human knowledge encounters insuperable difficulties in getting to the other side. The only viable option would appear to be that of constructing an "alternative" epistemology, a special way of knowing that might maneuver an end run around the strict criteria of rational knowing. The requests for such an alternative epistemology brought about the faith versus reason problematic. There soon developed a growing consensus that only faith can provide a direct access to the logos. But this faith continued to make purchases on the epistemological problematic and came to be defined as a form of belief.

In the shift to a semantics of the gift, there is a double deconstruction at work—a deconstruction of the metaphysical and the epistemological alike. Otherwise than being and otherwise than the logic of the epistemic, on the hither side of law, robustly aneconomic, transcending the culture spheres of science, morality, art, and religion itself, the gift continues to register its traces in our discourse and action as we respond to the otherness in the call of conscience and in the face of the neighbor. Gift-talk pervades our discourse, and we make gift giving a part of our lives. The gift comes to presence in the history of our praxial engagements and in this coming to presence makes itself known. This making itself known, however, is not a knowledge borne by an epistemology of recognition based on a metaphysical presence. But it is a knowledge nonetheless. Let us call it a knowledge informed by a "hermeneutic of acknowledgment as attestation."

The blurring of the grammar of acknowledgment with the grammar of recognition is one of the more glaring misdirections of modern epistemology. The epistemological turn, in search of the logos within the episteme, placed its bets on the resources of recognition, more specifically recognition through representation, to deliver trustworthy knowledge of ourselves and the world. An epistemology of recognition, within an economy of logic governed by rules either of a formal or transcendental sort, yearns for a representation of objectifiable contents as the foundation for knowledge. These laws and rules within the restricted economy of logic are laid out in advance of the event of knowing. Criteria for what counts as knowledge are front-loaded, supplied prior to the events of perception and conception.

Credit needs to be given to Hegel for his early discernment of certain unexamined presuppositions that travel with an epistemology of recognition that front-loads the determinations of what might count as knowledge. If such were indeed to be the case, then one would have to know how to swim before entering the pool, one would have to master the game of chess before approaching the board, one would have to know the rules of etiquette before encountering other selves. Considerations of this sort prompted Hegel to define the dialectic of self-consciousness and consciousness of other selves in terms of an adventure of "acknowledgment." "Self-consciousness," Hegel writes, "is in and for itself by virtue of its being for another self-consciousness; that is to say, it occurs only as acknowledged (*als ein Anerkanntes*)."[7] It is quite clear that Hegel, at least at this stage of his philosophical development, placed considerable weight on the dynamics of acknowledgment (*Anerkennung*) in the dialectics of self-knowledge and knowledge of other selves. It is unfortunate that the English translation of the passage at issue renders the German *Anerkennung* as *recognition,* thus obscuring Hegel's own distinction between knowing in the process of acknowledging and the abstract cognition that informs recognition and representation.

To be sure, Hegel himself may be partly responsible for this unfortunate translation, given the turn in his later works to a subject-centered edifice of absolute knowledge, which swallowed the concrete dialectics of consciousness of self and other selves that he had articulated in his earlier writings. This is one of the developments in the "wrong turn" taken by Hegel, by virtue of which he became one of the progenitors of modern epistemology. Nonetheless, the lesson to be learned from Hegel's *Phenomenology* is that one need be wary about having the logos

---

7. "Das Selbstbewusstsein ist an und für sich, indem and dadurch, dass es für ein anderes an und für sich ist: d.h. es ist nur als ein Anerkanntes," G. W. F. Hegel, *Phänomenologie des Geistes,* Philosophische Bibliothek, Sechste Auflage (Hamburg: Verlag von Felix Meiner, 1952), 141.

of acknowledgment slide into a logic of recognition—in spite of the fact that Hegel himself failed to live up to his earlier insights.

The limitation within an epistemology of recognition for addressing the logic of the gift has to do mainly with its heavy investment in the grammar of "re-presentation," negotiating a "re-turn" to an original source—a primal presentation or a founding principle. Various internal criticisms of the principle of representation (internal within the designs of epistemological inquiry) have of course appeared from time to time. The determination of that which is "present" and that which is "re-presented" appears to suffer perpetual deferral due to the dearth of trustworthy signifiers. These difficulties become intensified when one aligns the logic of the gift with a representational theory of knowledge. The logic of the gift knows no such return to and representation of a primal source, for any such return would be an annihilation of the gift as gift.

The epistemology of recognition is oriented backward, seeking a recovery of a present in the past. The hermeneutics of acknowledgment is oriented forward, searching for intimations of the possible in the future. It is only the hermeneutics of acknowledgment that is able to disclose the dynamics of the gift as ceaselessly centrifugal, always proceeding outward, never returning to the center—lest it lose its dynamics of a giving without expectation of return. This enables one to proceed beyond the alleged aporia of thanking someone for a gift without returning something to the giver and consequently annulling the gift as gift. Within the confines of this alleged aporia, acknowledging the gift with a thank-you transforms the gift into a commodity that one then returns to the giver. The thank-you becomes the repayment for the gift.

But thanking, expressing gratitude, need not remain within the strictures of an economy of exchange relations. It is precisely this that Nietzsche failed to grasp, because he confined gratitude within the economy of the will-to-power. Within such an economy, gratitude is destined to become a subtle form of enslavement, and love can never become more than a coefficient of pity. Acknowledging a gift is indeed a *response*, illustrating the ethical moment of a "fitting response," but not every response is a *return*—a recompense, a reward, remuneration, or reparation, somehow circling back to the giver.

Let us suppose that to acknowledge a gift is not to return something to the giver but rather to give to the other—to the third person, the neighbor, to the one who is nearby, both in physical and social space, and thus *continue* the giving. One acknowledges a former mentor by thanking him or her for the gift of knowledge not by returning something within the centripetal economy of repayment but rather by becoming a mentor for others within a centrifugal space of reaching out to the other. This defines the centrifugal nature of the gift, moving away from the center as the giver, moving outward to the third party, and eventually to all citizens of the wider polis. It is in this manner that giving is perpetuated as an expenditure without return, enhancing the quality of life among the inhabitants of the earth in a drive toward justice and social solidarity.

It is a hermeneutic of acknowledgment rather than an epistemology of recognition that offers resources for identifying the logos of the gift and the manner of its presence in giving and receiving. Acknowledging includes in its dynamics an "attesting." It comports a testimony, testifying of a presence or a trace of a presence, deploying a discernment that exceeds the criteria of the restricted economy of recognition. One acknowledges the unconditionality of the gift of *agapē,* a love that expects nothing in return, by attesting to it. Paul Ricoeur is helpful on this point when he writes: "Attestation presents itself first, in fact, as a kind of belief. But it is not a doxic belief, in the sense in which *doxa* (belief) has less standing than *epistēmē* (science, or better, knowledge). Whereas doxic belief is implied in the grammar of 'I believe-that,' attestation belongs to the grammar of 'I believe-in.' It thus links up with testimony, as the etymology reminds us, inasmuch as it is the speech of the one giving testimony that one believes."[8] Although the very grammar of belief itself may well become increasingly problematic as one moves along, Ricoeur's distinction between "believing-that" and "believing-in" helps to advance the cause. I believe *in* my friend, and in my believing *in* him I attest to his trustworthiness. And this believing-in overrides any believing-that predicated on the basis of observations by disinterested parties. Indeed, I am able to believe *in* my friend *in spite of* beliefs by others *that* he is unreliable. We can thus see how the family resemblance of "acknowledgment," "attestation," "testimony," and "trust" is set forth in the logos of the gift.

The gift as logos, acknowledged and attested to as unconditional love, becomes incarnate. Although itself aneconomic, it enters the economy of intersubjective transactions. It is wholly other in its Levinasian "absolute exteriority"; yet it makes its presence known in the face of the orphan, the widow, and the stranger. Converging with the finite and the conditioned, the gift refuses to become coincident with the finite and the conditioned. Convergence without coincidence, conjuncture without identity—such is the dynamics of the gift in human affairs. Hence,

---

8. Paul Ricoeur, *Oneself as Another,* trans. Kathleen Blamey (Chicago: University of Chicago Press, 1992), 21.

one is able to speak of the logos that was the gift from time immemorial, becoming flesh and dwelling among us, as transversal. Convergence with a restricted economy without coincidence and identity, retaining the integrity of difference, the gift informs our thought, discourse, and action. Older than the metaphysical binary of the universal versus the particular, the logos of the gift is *trans-versal* rather than *uni-versal,* present in the particularities of historical becoming without absorption into the episodical and historically-specific. *Trans*historical but not *a*historical, the logos has the resources to transcend the economy of accumulated values and traditional institutions and project possibilities for the giving of gifts yet to unfold.[9]

The gift that is the logos is also the "kairos." In the concept of the kairos, we encounter another contribution of the Greeks that made a decisive impact upon subsequent Western modes of thought. In addressing the perplexing problem of time the Greeks saw fit to distinguish kairos from chronos, the qualitative time of lived experience from the objectively measured time of chronometers, clocks, and calendars. There is within the economy of time itself the difference of a time that measures the movement of objects across space with respect to before and after and a time that marks out the "hour" of decision, the "right" time, the "opportune moment" for executing a plan of action. After Aristotle provided us with his celebrated definition of time in his *Physics* as the measurement of *kinesis* within a scheme of coordinates of earlier and later, he introduced the notion of the kairos in his *Ethics* to give an account of the qualitative temporality that indicates the right time for the actualization of the virtues.

The pivotal importance of the role of the kairos in Western philosophy and theology, from the early church fathers to medieval theology to modern philosophy and beyond, is hard to overestimate. From the New Testament narrative of Christ's coming *en kairo* to Nietzsche's appropriation of the notion to flesh out his concept of the "hour of fate" as the great moment in the life of the Overman, one finds a variegated landscape of usages. It was Kierkegaard, however, who may well be responsible for giving the notion its most decisive expression in the

9. For an extended discussion on the concept of transversality as it relates to the dynamics of reason within the economy of communicative praxis, see Schrag, *The Resources of Rationality,* particularly chap. 6, "Transversal Rationality," 148–79. See also van Huyssteen's highly illuminating application of the concept of transversality in framing the notion of a postfoundationalist rationality that is able to address the relation between science and theology in such a way that circumvents both the foundationalist rationality of modernity and the rejection of rationality in postmodernity, *The Shaping of Rationality.*

philosophical and theological literature of modernity. The concept of the kairos supplies the centerpiece for *Philosophical Fragments* and plays a major role in Kierkegaard's doctrine of the "stages along life's way"— the aesthetical, the ethical, and the religious: "And now the moment. Such a moment has a peculiar character. It is brief and temporal indeed, like every moment; it is transient as all moments are; it is past, like every moment in the next moment. And yet it is decisive, and filled with the eternal. Such a moment ought to have a distinctive name; let us call it the *Fullness of Time.*"[10]

This consolidation of the pivotal importance of the moment in *Philosophical Fragments* needs to be understood in conjunction with the role of the religious stage, more aptly named the religious existence-sphere, as articulated in *Concluding Unscientific Postscript.* The religious existence-sphere has two levels or dimensions—religiousness A and religiousness B. Religiousness A is the religion of immanence, religion within the limits of an existential dialectics, religion as an intramundane culture-sphere alongside the culture-spheres of science, morality, and art. Religiousness B marks a rupture of immanence and an accentuation of alterity and asymmetry in the divine-human relationship: "In religiousness B the edifying is a something outside the individual—the individual does not find the edification by finding the God-relationship within himself, but relates himself to something outside himself to find the edification."[11] Here we find an unambiguous emphasis on the alterity, exteriority, and primacy in the God-relationship. The presence of the Deity breaks in from the "outside"; and it breaks in at the decisive moment in the "Fullness of Time." It is at this juncture, against the backdrop of the acknowledgment of the kairotic moment, that we find the answer to Climacus's question that runs throughout both *Philosophical Fragments* and *Concluding Unscientific Postscript:* How can something historical become decisive for an eternal happiness?

The narrative of the eternal becoming historical in the moment of decision brings us to a crucial scenario in the workings of the gift as at once logos and kairos, determining the manner of presence that is at issue in the grammar of incarnation. The logos as incarnate in the flesh of historical becoming *presents itself,* comes to mind, is set forth in the moment as the locus of historical decision as one answers to the call of alterity in the visage of the neighbor. The gift as kairos defines the special

10. Søren Kierkegaard, *Philosophical Fragments or A Fragment of Philosophy,* trans. David F. Swenson (Princeton, N.J.: Princeton University Press, 1936), 13.

11. Søren Kierkegaard, *Concluding Unscientific Postscript,* trans. David F. Swenson (Princeton, N.J.: Princeton University Press, 1941), 498.

times and places for gift giving, the right moment for a gift to be given and to be received. And, if for only at the moment, the gift is outside the economy of distribution and exchange, sans anticipation of return and reward. And if the gift is indeed, as attested to by the author of I John, the eternal gift of love, then we will have made some inroads into solving Kierkegaard's riddle of how one can live in eternity while one hears the hall clock strike.

In the torturous development of the history of philosophy, and particularly in the West, vibrant notions of the logos and the kairos as gift suffered the fate of entanglement within a metaphysical and epistemological logocentrism. The logos became an abstract and universal structure of rationality, encompassing the scale of being from the lowest to the highest, making possible the adequation of the intellect with its proper objects of knowledge. Kairos suffered the destiny of suffocation within an abstract spatio-temporal coordinate in which temporality limps along as a fourth dimension of space.[12]

One of the singular contributions of Heidegger in his monumental *Being and Time* was that of a deconstruction of the metaphysical edifices that buttressed the concept of time in its Western development. Moving out from a hermeneutically based analytic of *Dasein*, Heidegger was able to secure an existential-ontological understanding of time that refused to be submerged by the categorial constraints of a metaphysics of quantifiable time. To be sure, it is not that measured chronological time is in itself a mistake. It displays its own legitimacy, avers Heidegger. The mistake resides in "mis-taking" objectively measured time for the time of lived experience, cosmological time for phenomenological time. The temporality of *Dasein*, with the entwinement of its three "ecstasies"—future, past, and present—is qualitatively distinct from time as the measurement of the movement of objects and things across an extended abstract spatial continuum. The ecstatic unity of coming-toward, having-been, and making-present—which characterizes time as it is experienced

---

12. Edward S. Casey in his two volumes *Getting Back into Place: Toward a Renewed Understanding of the Place-World* (Bloomington: Indiana University Press, 1993) and *The Fate of Place: A Philosophical History* (Berkeley: University of California Press, 1997) has been able to rescue time from its subordination to space while rescuing qualitatively apprehended place from its reduction to quantitatively determined space. The lived concreteness of place suffers disfigurement when comprehended within the abstracted coordinates of geometrical space. With detailed, intricate, and imaginative phenomenological analysis and description, for which Casey is internationally recognized, he shows in these volumes how the presence of place is best understood as an abode or dwelling that is constitutive of our lived experience, the locus of an embodiment that is infused with remembrance.

in our communicative practices—resists reduction to a serialization of abstracted point-like nows.

In Heidegger's recovery of the lived time of human existence, the moment (*Augenblick*) takes on a distinct privilege. It is the moment that provides the locus for decision, and it is in deciding that *Dasein* is able to achieve a unification of its three temporal ecstasies, grasping the present as it recalls its past in its projective orientation toward the future. Such is the ecstatic unity of the being of *Dasein*, making possible the meeting of the past and the future in the "presence" of the moment. This presence, however, it needs be emphasized, is not the "now-point" (*Jetzt-punkt*) of cosmological time—a present that remains forever a specious present that can never be grasped nor recovered. The moment is the present as an "existential now," the right time for deliberation and action. Heidegger's *Augenblick* appears to be very much like "the moment" that played such a pivotal role in the thought of Kierkegaard.

Yet there is a difference between Kierkegaard and Heidegger's understanding of the moment that has some notable consequences. Heidegger's *Augenblick* is Kierkegaard's moment as the kairotic "fullness of time" at once secularized and ontologized. There is indeed much that follows from this. Heidegger's philosophy, particularly that of the early period, can be read as a secularization and ontologization of the concrete existential reflections by Kierkegaard. Heidegger's "universal phenomenological ontology," as sketched in his *Being and Time*, tells the story of how Kierkegaard's ethical- and religious-oriented understanding and use of *existence* can be transposed into an ontological/existential key. The basic vocabularies of the two thinkers exhibit striking similarities. In the writings of both philosophers one finds consecutive attention given to the phenomena of anxiety, conscience, guilt, the moment, decision, death, and time. But whereas Kierkegaard understood these notions in their concrete ethical and religious expression, Heidegger ontologized them in the interests of devising a fundamental ontology that lays out the universal ontological-existential structure of Dasein.[13]

Given such a preoccupation with the ontological and the existential (*existenzial*), after having subjected the ontic and the concrete existentiell (*existenziell*) to a phenomenological *epochē*, it is of course not surprising that Heidegger avoids the ethical and the religious as specific topics of inquiry. Heidegger's assessment of Kierkegaard's contribution is not particularly laudatory. In *Being and Time* he writes somewhat disparag-

13. For a consecutive and detailed investigation of Heidegger's secularization and ontologization of Kierkegaard's concrete existential elucidations, see Schrag, *Existence and Freedom*.

ingly of Kierkegaard for not being able to raise his discussion of anxiety to an ontological level. In *Holzwege* his tone is even more disparaging. Kierkegaard, he tells us here, "is not a thinker, but rather a religious writer."[14] However, as we have already had occasion to observe, new paths of inquiry open as one proceeds from Heidegger I to Heidegger II to Heidegger III. In the maneuver of the first *Kehre,* the focus shifts from the "meaning of Being " to the "truth of Being" and from language as an articulation of the intelligibility of the care-structure to language as the "house of Being." In the second *Kehre,* the shift appears to be even more dramatic in its proposal for an erasure, a crossing out of Being, suggesting that the inquiry into being formulated against the backdrop of the ontological/ontic difference has now exhausted its resources and that it is time to move on.

And it is the question of where one moves to in moving beyond the question of being, the ontological/ontic difference, the existential structures of *Dasein,* and language as the "house of Being," that would appear to be of some importance. What comes after fundamental ontology has fulfilled its delimited purpose? Who comes after *Dasein*? How might the ethical and the religious question be re-asked? Heidegger has repeatedly informed us that if he were to write a theology the word *being* would not appear. He has not favored us with writing such a theology. Might it be too bold to suggest that if one were to reclaim ethical and religious issues after ontological/existential analysis has run its course, something like a return to the concrete existentiell notions of Kierkegaard would come into view? Would a return to a Kierkegaardian attestation of the kairos as the fullness of time on the existentiell plane, after its ontologization as the *Augenblick* by Heidegger whereby it becomes part of the furniture of universal phenomenological ontology has served its purpose, possibly bring a new vision of the aneconomic gift within the economy of intra-mundane transactions? Plainly enough, such a vision would open up an invitation to a fitting response, a fitting response that keeps the gift as its measure.

The Gift and the Fitting Response

The delimitation of ontology led us to ethics. The delimitation of ethics pointed us in the direction of the gift. The gift, we were soon to discover,

14. Martin Heidegger, "Kierkegaard ist kein Denker, sondern ein religioser Schrift-steller," *Holzwege* (Frankfurt am Main: Vittorio Klostermann, 1950), 230.

surpasses both ontic and ontological determinants. It is not only other-wise than the structures of being, it is also otherwise than the *nomos* that governs the economy of ethical transactions. The gift as logos transcends the economy of reciprocating exchange relations in our personal and public life. We found also, however, that the gift is kairos, that which is given at the right time, at the opportune moment, destined to take on the flesh of ethical responsibility, presenting us with the paradox of gift giving within the ethos of civil society.

The question about the ethical is thus foreordained to return after its delimitation and suspension. An acknowledgment of the gift as logos and kairos is at once a call for an ethic of the fitting response. A gift becomes a genuine gift, an event yearning for fulfillment and oriented toward actualization, only when there is an acknowledgment and re-sponse on the part of the receiver of the gift. Responsibility is implicated in the gift event. This leads us back to the ethical. But we are not back to the ethical in the way that we were in the ethical prior to its suspension as *nomos* or law defined teleologically, deontologically, or in a utilitarian manner. The ethical is now understood as transfigured by the gift as its proper content and measure. Clearly, we continue to define ends for human action, legislate duties and rights, and speculate about that which is good for the greatest number. We continue to traffic within an economy of goods and services that make up the ethical fabric of civil so-ciety. Like Abraham of old, we again have our Isaac after the teleological suspension, but we do not "have" him in the same way. "Having" is itself transfigured, shorn of it its individualized possessiveness. Ends, duties, rights, and goods are reclaimed and themselves become gifts that temper and transfigure the configurations of reciprocal exchange relations that remain beholden to the constraints of laws of distribution.

The abstract reciprocity and reversibility that defines social dynam-ics and systems of justice is tempered by an acknowledgment of the asym-metry that always travels with the gift, indicating that any ethic of rights and duties needs find its initiating catalyst in an ethic of care that has *caritas* as its content and measure—a caring that expects no return. The grammar of "asymmetrical reciprocity," which has been brought into prominence by Iris Marion Young and Patricia J. Huntington, is particu-larly helpful for explicating the dynamics of the ethical as the paradoxical intersection of the aneconomic and the asymmetrical with the condi-tions for reciprocity and reversibility.[15] The vocabulary of asymmetrical

---

15. See particularly Iris Marion Young, "Asymmetrical Reciprocity: On Moral Respect, Wonder, and Enlarged Thought," *Constellations: An International Journal of Critical and Demo-*

reciprocity provides a conceptual sheet anchor against a fusing of self and other in the ethical relation, occluding the "otherness" of the other. It furnishes a communicative space of discourse and action that allows for a proper distancing of self from the other, avoiding the positional identity that is endemic within an ethical intersubjectivity grounded on an untrammeled reciprocity that privileges the cognitive act of empathic identification. I can never fully empathize with the psyche of another self, and the other self can never fully empathize with my psyche, short of foisting alien thoughts, desires, and needs onto each.

Personal histories and social roles are simply too complex for such reciprocity and reversibility. Iris Young states it well when she observes that social positions are inherently asymmetrical and "cannot be plucked from their contextualized relations and substituted for one another." And Patricia Huntington, following certain suggestions by Young, sums up the matter quite nicely when she writes: "A model of asymmetrical reciprocity, not reversibility, maintains the space requisite to work toward enlarged thinking. . . . In that definite social space, overlapping histories and social positions meet but with remainder."[16]

The lesson to be learned from the suggestive notion of asymmetrical reciprocity is that living in civil society with its moral demands requires a task of mediation without identity, convergence without coincidence, acknowledging the presence of an asymmetrical gift within an economy of reciprocity. After the suspension of the law of distribution and exchange with its distributive justice and its call for substitutability and equality, enabling a vision of the gift sans repayment in kind, one finds oneself in a transvalued economy, where things are not the same as they were before. We continue to ask the questions, What is my telos? What is my duty? What are my civil rights? and What is the social good? but we now ask these questions against the backdrop of a wider scheme of things that solicits a fitting response. And this wider scheme of things has much to do with the acknowledgment of a gift that antedates our thought and action—a gift that informs the very definitions of telos, duties, rights, and aspirations for that which is good for the polis.

The responding self remains situated in a span of tension between the aneconomic event of the gift and the demands of ethical life in civil society. In the wake of the suspension of the teleological and deontological norms of our social existence, enabling us to acknowledge

cratic Theory, 3: 340–63; and Patricia J. Huntington, Ecstatic Subjects, Utopia, and Recognition: Kristeva, Heidegger, Irigaray (Albany: State University of New York Press, 1998) chap. 8, "Asymmetrical Reciprocity."

16. Young, "Asymmetrical Reciprocity," 352–53; Huntington, Ecstatic Subjects, 301.

the alterity and asymmetry of gift giving, the norms are reclaimed as it were and assume new roles in the structure and dynamics of personal and public life. We proceed to draw up policies concerning fairness and justice, duties and rights, goods and obligations, but we no longer draw them up in isolation from their relation to the gift. These policies are now transvalued by virtue of a gift giving that transcends and relativizes all particularized normative claims. The principles of reciprocity that inform the definitions of justice and individual rights are transfigured and vitalized by a protoethic of care, in which the fitting response is to perpetuate the event of giving.

An imaginative theological spin on the asymmetry-reciprocity dyad is found in Stephen Webb's provocative little volume with the suggestive title *The Gifting God*. As an exercise in theological deconstruction, the central argument unfolds as an analysis of the concept of the Trinity into a "Gifting God" who is both excessive and reciprocal. Excess and reciprocity are understood in terms of their co-implication. "My governing insight," writes Webb, "is the following: *divine excess begets reciprocity*. Without excess, reciprocity becomes calculation, bartering, exchange; without reciprocity, excess becomes irrelevant, anarchic, and wasteful. . . . In the end, what God gives is the power of giving itself, the possibility that we can all participate in the movement of giving with the hope that such generosity will be enhanced, organized, and consummated in God's very own becoming."[17] God as the Divine Gift, in its trinitarian expression as at once the Giver the Given and the Giving, imparts the power of giving itself, calling one to the challenge of perpetuating the event of giving, acknowledging the excess of the gift as one reciprocates by creating more and more giving in responding to the challenges of our civic responsibilities.

Is there a vocabulary adequate to the task of aligning the acknowledgment and response concerning matters of the gift with the establishment of directives for shaping the institutions and culture spheres of our sociohistorical existence? What configurations do our discourses and our actions assume in response to the kairotic moment of the gift? What informs and gives substance to our talk about friendship, community, and political goals that might auger in the direction of a participatory democracy? How does the gift, whose proper locus and origin is otherwise than the *nomos* that structures the economy of civil society, make its presence felt in the concrescence of the mundane culture spheres? With these questions we approach certain formidable challenges.

---

17. Stephen H. Webb, *The Gifting God: A Trinitarian Ethics of Excess* (New York: Oxford University Press, 1996), 90–91.

Jacques Derrida has addressed some of the concerns at stake in these issues in his thought-provoking *Politics of Friendship*. In this essay he sets the discussion against the backdrop of the entwinement of the concepts of gift, friendship, and politics as these concepts bear on the future of democracy. He finds it particularly distressing that the concept of friendship has become so closely allied with the concept of fraternity. The solidification of these two concepts into an unbroken solidarity is destined to produce an exclusionary democracy of "fraternal friendship" in which feminine and heterosexual friendships are denied a space in which to thrive. Hence, what needs to be put on the agenda, according to Derrida, is an experimentation with a new notion of friendship, one that will integrate the concepts of the gift and justice into a vibrant and more inclusive democracy.

Achieving such an inclusive democracy, however, requires overcoming some formidable impediments along the way. "Is it possible," muses Derrida, "to think and to implement democracy, that which would keep the old name 'democracy', while uprooting from all the figures of friendship (philosophical and religious) which prescribe fraternity: the family and the androcentric ethnic group?"[18] Clearly, to implement such a democracy the range and reach of friendship will need to be decisively expanded. It will need to move beyond all homofraternal confines; it will need to include the sorority of wives and widows, single mothers, lesbian and heterosexual partners. But there is an even more resilient obstacle that stands in the way of actualizing such a vibrant and inclusive democracy, and this has to do with certain inherent limitations within the concept of friendship itself. And nowhere does this become more evident than when one turns one's attention to the aporia in the alleged connection of friendship with the gift.

The gift of friendship circulates within the parameters of a restricted economy. This was already quite apparent in the Greek concept of friendship as *philia*, a friendship based on conditions of reciprocity. *Philia* is a love that expects something commensurate in return and is possible only between equals. One cannot be a friend to everyone. One has friends, says Aristotle, so that one can find in them qualities of character with which one can identify and which contribute to a reciprocating fulfillment. Friendship requires an interaction and exchange with equals, borne by relations of symmetry and reciprocity wherewith to achieve a mutual perfectibility of virtue on the path to self-realization. It

18. Jacques Derrida, *The Politics of Friendship*, trans. George Collins (New York: Verso Press, 1997), 306.

is not surprising that this aristocratic ideal, which permeated so much of Greek thought, should also figure in the Greek concept of friendship and in the end tip the scales in the direction of a preference for aristocracy over democracy. Given such a disposition, to speak of being friends with one's enemies would be for the Greek mind nothing short of a blatant oxymoron.

It was thus, avers Derrida, that the Christian doctrine of love as presented in the New Testament narrative appeared on the scene as such an affront to the Greek ideal, at once transforming the notion of fraternity into a universal brotherhood and setting the conditions for the commandment to love even one's enemies: "One becomes a brother, in Christianity, one is worthy of the eternal father, only by loving one's enemy as one's neighbor or as oneself." Here the gift of love, transcending all economies of exchange relations, is somehow to be made efficacious within the transactions of civil society: "One would thus have to think the dissymmetry of a gift without exchange, therefore an infinite one—infinitely disproportionate, in any case, however modest it may be, from the vantage point of terrestrial finitude."[19] At this juncture in the narrative, it would indeed appear that the very concept of Christian love must remain an impossible ideal and bereft of any relevance to the economies of civil society.

It is difficult to find a philosopher in the history of Christian thought who has agonized more over the aporia that travels with the incarnation of the gift of love in the bowels of terrestrial finitude than has Søren Kierkegaard. His brilliant and profound *Works of Love* places this issue into the foreground. Using the New Testament commandment, "You shall love your neighbor as yourself," as the lynchpin of his narrative, Kierkegaard carries through a disciplined and consecutive hermeneutic on the movement of intercalating senses across the landscapes of "neighbor," "love," "you shall," and "as yourself." What we learn from all this is, first of all, that the concept of the neighbor is expanded to include every other self in its situationality of being "near-by," incorporating differences in regard to gender, ethnicity, wealth, and social status: "Every human being is the neighbor. In being king, beggar, rich man, poor man, male, female, etc., we are not like each other—therein we are indeed different. But in being the neighbor we are all unconditionally like each other. Dissimilarity is temporality's method of confusing that marks every

19. Ibid., 285, 286.

human being differently, but the neighbor is eternity's mark—on every human being."[20]

We also learn from the commandment that the quality of love at issue extends beyond the friend-enemy distinction. My enemy is also one who is near-by, and by his presence he solicits my love as much as does my friend: "Therefore the one who truly loves the neighbor loves also his enemy. The distinction *friend* or *enemy* is difference in the object of love, but love for the neighbor has the object that is without difference. The neighbor is the utterly unrecognizable dissimilarity between persons or is the eternal equality before God—the enemy, too, has this equality."[21] Clearly, it is this expression of love, overriding the distinction between friend and enemy, that Derrida has in mind when he speaks of the "dissymmetry of a gift without exchange" and of the gift of love as being "infinitely disproportionate . . . from the vantage point of terrestrial finitude."

Plainly enough, Kierkegaard is in the background whenever there is talk about the disproportionality of the gift of love from the vantage point of the economies of civil society. This is underscored in Kierkegaard's teaching on the self-sacrificing quality of the gift of love: "The inwardness of love must be self-sacrificing and therefore without requirement of any reward . . . It has no reward, not even that of being loved."[22] Yet, as Kierkegaard was profoundly aware given his sensitivities to the ambiguities of human motivation, there can be no pure self-sacrifice. Even self-sacrifice issues from motivations that are never wholly liberated from self-interest.

This accentuation of love as a gift without exchange, a love that seeks no reward, provides the backdrop for Kierkegaard's rather firm distinction between erotic love and friendship on the one hand and the love of one's neighbor on the other hand: "The object of both erotic love and friendship has preference's name, 'the beloved,' 'the friend,' who is loved in contrast to the whole world. The doctrine, on the contrary, is to love the neighbor, to love the whole human race, all people, even the enemy, and not to make exceptions, neither of preference nor of aversion. . . . Erotic love (*Elskov*) is defined by the object; friendship is defined by the object; only love for the neighbor is defined by love (*Kjerlighed*)."[23] What is in play in Kierkegaard's hermeneutical typology of the different

---

20. Søren Kierkegaard, *Works of Love,* ed. and trans. Howard V. Hong and Edna H. Hong (Princeton, N.J.: Princeton University Press, 1995), 89.

21. Ibid., 67–68.

22. Ibid., 130–31.

23. Ibid., 19, 66.

kinds of love, setting eros and friendship in contradistinction to love of one's neighbor, are distinctions that revert back to both early Greek and early Christian thought. The Greek language bequeathed a legacy of distinctions not only between sensual love (*epithymia*) and friendship (*philia*), but also between these two and *eros*.

Philia is love of a friend; *eros*, specifically as portrayed in Plato's *Symposium*, is intellectual love, love not of things beautiful but of the eternal form of beauty; and *epithymia* is love as exemplified in the wayward passions of the human soul. In subsequent usage, *eros* and *epithymia* became closely allied and at times viewed as virtually identical. It is this substitution of the one for the other that is in play in Kierkegaard's grammar of "erotic love." The principal point at issue, however, turns on Kierkegaard's characterization of both *eros* and *philia* as forms of love within an economy of exchange relations. Symmetry and reciprocity are the necessary conditions for their fruition and continuation. They are preferential, possessive, and conditional. As such they are to be contrasted with what in the New Testament is named *agapē*, later to be translated by the Latin *caritas*, providing the touchstone for Saint Augustine's doctrine of ethics. It is within this historical context that Kierkegaard's explication of the commandment, "You shall love your neighbor as yourself," needs to be understood. And here, one is indeed dealing with love as a giving without return, abridging the rules of symmetry and reciprocity, a love that is nonpreferential, nonpossessive, and unconditional —a love that loves for the sake of loving and is indeed able to love *in spite of* remaining unrequited.

Such a love, in the guise of a gift that expects nothing in return, outside the bounds of the economy of reciprocal social transactions, appears to have all of the features of an impossible ideal, given the fragility of the human condition. To expect from this impossible ideal certain moral imperatives for the attainment of justice in civil society is an expectation that seems destined for disappointment. What possible bearing can all this have on the political demands of our age? Both Derrida and Kierkegaard, albeit from different perspectives, would assent to the impossibility of that which they have so eloquently described in their discourses on the gift. Indeed, Derrida repeatedly makes much of the impossibility of the gift. The interior dynamics of giving a gift is such that it engenders the destruction of the gift as gift. The gift is annihilated in the moment it is given and received.

All this makes the applicability of the gift, and more precisely the gift of love without expectation of return, to political life peculiarly problematic. Here it would seem that any "politics of friendship" is doomed always to come up short. If there is to be any talk about a democracy that is somehow leavened by the gift, it will need to be about a democracy in the future. Derrida is explicit in making this point: "For democracy remains to come; this is its essence in so far as it remains: not only will it remain indefinitely perfectible, hence always insufficient and future, but, belonging to the time of the promise, it will always remain, in each of its future times, to come: even when there is democracy, it never exists, it is never present, it remains the theme of a nonpresentable concept."[24] The incarnation of the gift into the economy of human affairs thus finds its fulfillment (if indeed the grammar of fulfillment is appropriate within this context) in an eschatological vision rather than in a political platform. Democracy is a gift always yet to unfold in the future and never an institutional model recovered from the past. Democracy, and the justice that undergirds it, is yet to come—and indeed always yet to come.

Both Kierkegaard and Derrida situate the temporality of the gift within an eschatological and messianic horizon. The commandment to love one's neighbor as one's self has not yet come to fulfillment in the economy of historical becoming. Likewise, for Derrida the gift of a politics of friendship with its justice and equality for all is yet to be actualized. It is the messianic, proclaims Derrida, or more precisely "*messianicity* without *messianism*" that provides "the opening to the future or to the coming of the other as the advent of justice."[25] Kierkegaard and Derrida thus seem to be in solid agreement that the Kingdom of God is a reality projected into the future. It has not yet come. As the culmination of an aneconomic gift that expects nothing in return, the Kingdom of God is *jenseits* rather than *dieseits*. It testifies of the gulf that separates the face and the voice of the infinite from the strivings of a fragile finite self. Yet, in the passion of both Kierkegaard and Derrida, we can discern a fervor and zeal to embody the infinite demand in the economy of public affairs, embracing ethnic, racial, and gender differences. Kierkegaard makes much of "our duty to love the people we see" as an injunction that follows directly from the commandment to love one's neighbor as oneself, and he emphasizes time and again that love knows no preferences in our dealings with the rich and the poor, the exalted and the lowly, the healthy and the infirm, the male and the female, and even the friend and the enemy.

But how can a wholly transcendent and aneconomic gift, messianic in character, projected into the future, impact on the finite and economic

24. Derrida, *Politics of Friendship,* 306.
25. Jacques Derrida, "Faith and Knowledge," in *Religion,* ed. Jacques Derrida and Gianni Vattimo (Stanford, Calif.: Stanford University Press, 1998), 17.

plane of existence in the present? Does not the future in some sense have to become present? How can the gift of love become "works of love" in the rough and tumble of our personal and social existence? Herein, one might say, resides the rub. To address this rub, which indeed reaches far back into both the philosophical and theological traditions of Western thought, antedating the insights on the subject that Kierkegaard and Derrida have provided, we propose a thought experiment on "eschatological preenactment." As we have observed, for Kierkegaard and Derrida the matter of thought at issue requires an eschatological perspective. Traveling a patch of the road together with these two provocative hermeneuticists, we propose the notion of eschatological preenactment, holding fast to the messianic horizon, but redescribing and reinterpreting this horizon as that of a preenacted eschatology. And in this appeal and testimony, we purport to secure the protoethical dimension that supplies the dynamic of the ethic of the gift as it relates to the requirements of the fitting response.

Preenacted eschatology is able to do duty on two fronts as it were. It avoids the pitfalls of a realized eschatology that issues from a philosophy of identity and radical interiority, and it circumvents the problems of an utterly transcendent eschatology that proceeds from a philosophy of difference and absolute exteriority. The first interpretation, that of realized eschatology, for which Hegel must bear much of the responsibility, places the eschatological fulfillment in the depths of the present, within the interstices of the "eternal now," testifying of an event already fully actualized. Hegel's philosophy of identity, with its narrative of the mediation of the transcendent and universal with the immanent and particular provides much of the backdrop for reflections on eschatology as already realized. The religious symbol of the Incarnation supplies the decisive indicator for such an eschatology. The Messiah indeed has already come, ever present in the eternal now of historical becoming, reconciling the world unto himself, overcoming all estrangement of self with other through an epiphany of mutual acknowledgment.

The second interpretation, that of an eschatology of absolute exteriority, always in the future and never present, also has its sources in the history of philosophical and religious thought; however, it has found contemporary support in the reflections of Emmanuel Levinas. As the philosopher of absolute exteriority, radical alterity, and unmediated asymmetry, Levinas provides the counterpoint to all philosophies of identity. In his celebration of difference to the point of abjuring all relations of reciprocity in hearing the call of the other, he places an unusually heavy burden on the task of securing ethical resources for the present age. All

such resources are embodied in a Messiah who is "immemorial"—who
has not been present in a past, who is not present in an eternal now, and
who is not a future event that will become present at a later date.

Now if it should be the case that Hegel with his philosophy of
identity, mediation, and consummate reciprocity and Levinas with his
philosophy of alterity, absolute exteriority, and asymmetry mark out the
parameters of our discourse on the ethics of the gift within civil society, then we have no option other than that of splitting the difference.
Against Hegel: while acknowledging the importance of his emphasis on
the incarnation of the transcendent logos in the theater of historical
becoming and the implications of this for ethical existence in civil society,
we nonetheless reject his overtures to a philosophy of identity and the accompanying realized eschatology. Against Levinas: while acknowledging
the robust transcendence of the gift and conceding that the Kingdom of
God has not yet come, attesting to the futurity of the epiphany of justice
as that which unfolds only in the fullness of time, we nonetheless testify
of a goodness that can happen here and now in our quotidian personal
and cultural life. From this splitting of the difference between Hegel and
Levinas we are able to learn that *although the Kingdom of God has not yet
come, it has already begun to come, and it is always beginning to come.* This is
the truth of preenacted eschatology.

The Kingdom of God as the messianic event has neither enjoyed
fulfillment in the economy of civil society, nor does it remain wholly exterior and transcendent to it. In this paradoxical suspension between the
gift of eternity and the response of temporality, the Jewish and Christian
testimonies on the messianic event converge while retaining an integrity
of difference. The messianic event is always in the future. It has not yet
come, and its presence will always bear the marks of futurity. But this
futurity is always a coming-to-presence, enabling an efficacy of the gift
within the thickness of historical experience.

It is in the thought of Kierkegaard that the eventing of the gift
as a qualification of historical consciousness resonates with an existential concreteness—"existential" not as universal ontological structure but
rather as lived-through ethico-religious practice. The Kingdom of God
is manifested in the workings of the gift as the works of love. Here the
emphasis falls on the actional component of love. "Christian love is sheer
action," writes Kierkegaard. Love is efficacious only when it is translated
into works. Love is action. Love achieves its incarnation in the presence
of praxis, where it conjoins with hope. In a trenchant commentary on
I Corinthians, Kierkegaard elucidates the internal connection of love
with hope: "But love, which is greater than faith and hope, also takes

upon itself the work of hope, or takes upon itself hope, hoping for others, as a work."[26]

Love binds together a working or acting with a hoping or anticipating. As a result of this interconnection, love takes on an eschatological orientation. It is always projected into the future. But this hoping, this claim on an eschatological event, Kierkegaard emphasizes, is never a simple wishing, craving, or expecting. Wishing, craving, and expecting are time-bound states of mind within the circle of calculation, control, and prediction. Hope testifies of the power of the possible to transform and transfigure the restricted economy of fleeting desires that remain within the temporal sphere of exchange relations: "To hope relates to the future, to possibility, which in turn, unlike actuality, is always a duality, the possibility of advance or of retrogression, of rising or falling, of good or of evil. The eternal *is,* but when the eternal touches the temporal or is in the temporal, they do not meet each other in the *present,* because in that case the present would itself be the eternal. The present, the moment, is over so quickly that it actually does not exist; it is only the boundary and therefore is past, whereas the past is what is present. Therefore, when the eternal is in the temporal, it is in the future . . . or in possibility. The past is the actual, the future is the possible; eternally, the eternal is the eternal; in time, the eternal is the possible, the future."[27]

To love is to hope, to be projected into the future, to *exist* as possibility. And it is as possibility that the eternal becomes incarnate in the temporal. The locus of this incarnation, as we have already observed, is articulated by Kierkegaard as "the moment." But this moment is not a discrete and isolated now-point in the evanescent becoming of actuality; it is instead the coming to presence of the eternal in the future as the possible. It is here we find Kierkegaard's most concise statement on the eschatology of love. Here is his concrete elucidation of the messianic—which is in advance both of Heidegger's existential-ontological structure of an anticipatory "running ahead" (*vorlaufen*) and Derrida's separation of "messianicity" and "messianism."[28]

---

26. Kierkegaard, *Works of Love,* 98–99; 248.

27. Ibid., 249.

28. It would appear that Derrida's distinction between messianicity and messianism follows closely on the heels of Heidegger's distinctions between the ontological and the ontic and the existential and the existentiell. Messianicity is the form of the expected future coming, without any specified content. It is the structure of the coming of the other without the presence of the other. For Derrida there is no trace of the Messiah in the face of the stranger as is the case in Levinas's notion of "the God who comes to mind." Messianicity for Derrida

A contemporary version of a Kierkegaardian-like eschatological ethics has been developed in Ramsey Eric Ramsey's combinatory "ethics of relief" and "areligious religiosity." Ramsey fleshes out his project with what he calls the "twofold strategy of working and waiting," combining an ethical dynamics with an eschatological vision. The ethics of relief performs a double function. It affords "relief" from the current ills of society by bringing the flattened world of actuality into "relief" against the backdrop of incursive possibilities. These incursive possibilities suspend the fixed teleological determinants within the economy of actuality and auger into a future as the power of the possible. It is this that supplies the measure for the complementarity of working and waiting, in which working toward relief from social injustice is combined with an eschatological posture of hoping and waiting: "This twofold strategy of working and waiting can assist the critical theoretical project of an ethics of relief. As long as we are in history we shall not have total redemption. Redemption occurs at the end of history, as an origin of something other that it initiates. This thinking is future oriented without being teleological. Although any working may well have a telos, waiting only has a future."[29]

The future, the possible, and the eternal are entwined. Plainly enough, within such a scheme of things, possibility cannot be lower or inferior to actuality. Kierkegaard had already made this quite clear with his repeated reminders in *Concluding Unscientific Postscript* that the possible is higher than the actual. However, it is only in *Works of Love* that we see the full ethical and religious implications of this deconstruction of the metaphysical elevation of the actual above the possible. The entwinement of the future, the possible, and the eternal is most decisively and most dramatically illustrated in *Works of Love*. We are commanded to love our neighbor as oneself. Such a love proceeds by dint of a projection into a future fulfillment, informing the love of the neighbor as a preenactment of this fulfillment. This preenactment of what in its fullness of time resides in the future takes shape in the form of the fitting response.

---

takes on the coloring of an ontological/existential structural determinant abstracted from its ontic/existentiell content. Might this justify an inference that as Heidegger, at least in his early period of *Being and Time,* ontologized and secularized the ethico-religious thought of Kierkegaard, so Derrida ontologized and secularized the philosophy of Levinas?

29. Ramsey Eric Ramsey, "Communication and Eschatology: The Work of Waiting, an Ethics of Relief, and Areligious Religiosity," *Communication Theory,* 7:4 (1997), 145–46. See also Ramsey Eric Ramsey, *The Long Path to Nearness: A Contribution to a Corporeal Philosophy of Communication and the Groundwork for an Ethics of Relief* (Atlantic Highlands, N.J.: Humanities Press, 1998).

The fitting response, using the measure of the gift of love, responds by apprehending space as a habitat for deeds that can be done, concretely illustrated in random acts of kindness and mercy, in which one exemplifies the virtuous deed of a Good Samaritan, as well as in the collaborative social projects of selfless charity, institutionalized, for example, in the Habitat for Humanity program. Illustrations of charity—the exemplification of *caritas*—in our personal and social life continue to testify of the incarnation of the gift of love in the preenactment posture of the fitting response.

A particularly poignant illustration of an ethics of charity in an accentuated time of need is that of the saving of thousands of Jews from certain extinction during the oppressive Vichy regime, established at the time of the German occupation of France in World War II. The inhabitants of the small town of Le Chambon, under the leadership of pastor André Trocmé, collaborated in the hiding of thousands of Jews and thus kept them from the boxcars on their way to the death camps in Germany. The account of this deliverance can be found in Philip Hallie's soul-wrenching book, *Lest Innocent Blood Be Shed*. The subtitle of the book masterfully consolidates the guiding motif: *The Story of the Village of Le Chambon and How Goodness Happened There*. Goodness, in the guise of a sacrificial love that bartered nothing in return, was instantiated at Le Chambon. In this isolated village in Southern France, there was a display of a gift that was unconditional, with its reward residing in the act of its being given.[30]

The story of Le Chambon, and others like it, stands as a reminder of the need to consult local narratives and case studies to illustrate how the gift can be given and received and how goodness can happen and justice be done within the economy of our civil societies. Another illustration of the workings of the gift within sociopolitical space is that provided by Georges Bataille with his perspective on the wider significance of the Marshall Plan. Designed by the United States government in the interests of postwar European reconstruction, the plan offered financial assistance to certain countries that had been devastated by the war. Bataille's read of the plan is that it was a singular and unique economic experiment that provided a strategy for dealing with excess resources by means of a pure expenditure in which wealth was dispensed without return. The dynamics of the Marshall Plan exemplified a species of squandering, albeit within the constraints of international interests. Yet, given the fact that the national interests of the United States were also very much at stake, clearly

---

30. Philip P. Hallie, *Lest Innocent Blood Be Shed: The Story of the Village of Le Chambon and How Goodness Happened There* (New York: Harper and Row, 1979).

the Marshall Plan as a form of political and economic organization does not give as clear an example of the working of the gift in civil society as does the story of Le Chambon.[31]

Remembering always that discourse and action blend into one another, we are not surprised to find this to be the case in narratives about the gift. Stories told by givers and receivers of the gift provide testimony of the actions and transactions of the gift's workings. We thus come to understand that storytelling is inseparable from the eventing of the gift within the economy of our daily life. The gift becomes manifest more decisively in the throes of narrative disclosure and rhetorical showing than in demonstrative proofs and formal argumentation. The gift is an event rather than a being. Events are told rather than inferred. And the telling that occurs in narratives of the gift is that of an acknowledgment and attestation rather than a recognition and representation. Events are the stuff of narrative knowledge in advance of epistemological criteria and protocols.

Michael J. Hyde in his treatise on the call of conscience has illustrated the eventing of the gift in its rhetorical expression. Rhetoric, according to Hyde, needs to be properly understood as an interruption, an interruption of our flattened everyday existence, in which the epideictic function of rhetoric as setting forth and disclosing becomes prominent. Hyde's principal focus is on the continuing volatile euthanasia debate, and he has managed to consolidate poignant stories by those who because of unmitigated pain and suffering had to struggle with the profound ethical issue of the "right to die" as a live option for the alleviation of their misery. Hyde frames his format as an investigation of the call of conscience as a practice of rhetoric as it relates to the euthanasia debate. Using Heidegger and Levinas as pivots for his theoretical analysis of the call of conscience, he quickly turns to the world of practice, in which the call takes on the exigency of the suffering face, crying out with a Levinasian urgency, Where art thou? and soliciting a corresponding Levinasian response, Here I am! In the stories of the afflicted Hyde retells, we see this call of conscience issued time and again. The suffering face of the infirm speaks in an interrogative mode, and we all have a responsibility to hear and understand the question and to respond with the "life-giving gift of acknowledgment." Ensconced in the suffering face is "the power to give the gift," the gift of a suffering for all others, occasioning the ethical responsibility to acknowledge the gift in the announcement, Here I am.[32]

---

31. Georges Bataille, *The Accursed Share: An Essay on General Economy*, vol. 1, trans. Robert Hurley (New York: Zone Books, 1989), 169–90.

32. Michael J. Hyde, *The Call of Conscience: Heidegger and Levinas, Rhetoric and the Euthanasia Debate* (Columbia: University of South Carolina Press, 2001), 256. See also p. 258: "We

What stories such as that provided by Hallie and rhetorical exercises such as those proffered by Hyde teach us is that there are indeed motivations of ethical attitudes and actions that transcend all expectations of return. The significant spin-off from such endeavors of genuine charity on the personal and social level is a moderating effect on the forces and metaphors of production and consumption, distribution and exchange. Here we see how the gift is able to impact quite directly on the structures and dynamics of civil society. Love becomes incarnate in human affairs. The eternal requirement of unconditionality is preenacted in the temporal domain of historical becoming.

For this call of unconditionality to be heard in the rough and tumble of civil society, however, certain presuppositions about both self and society need to be brought into question—presuppositions having to do with the senses of "owness" and "ownership" as they are in play both in the regulative principles of social organization and in the dynamics of self-understanding and self-constitution. Informed by a semantics of possession and dispossession, excess and expenditure, surplus and squandering, debt and repayment within the restricted economy of a market society, the taken-for-granted assumption is that gifts are commodities that first have to be owned. Thus gift giving immediately gravitates into a transaction of gift exchange and makes sense only against the backdrop of a concept of private property. Rights of private property undergird the privilege of giving. To be able to dispossess oneself of something, to give something away, presupposes a condition of prior possession or ownership, all of which would seem to lead to the somewhat curious conclusion that only those who are privileged by ownership of private property are truly able to give.

But suppose we question this basic presupposition. Perhaps the goods that are circulating in our social practices are never strictly one's own. Perhaps the very notions of strict ownership and absolute possession are slippery eels. Perhaps the goods we appropriate from nature and through our sundry projects of making are themselves "gifts," of which we are the stewards or custodians but never absolute owners. Perhaps a semantics of stewardship is more appropriate than is the grammar of property rights and private ownership for understanding the efficacy of the gift in civil society. It may well be that the principal error of those who analyze the gift back into a framework of excess and expenditure, possession and dispossession, granting a privilege to the private over

have a need to be needed, to be both the sender and receiver of the life-giving gift of acknowledgment."

the public, is to fail to acknowledge that objects that are given as gifts never issue from a zero-point origin of absolute ownership. The goods of the earth and the services of humankind can indeed be "privatized," but before this occurs, they transcend the claims for inviolable property rights. To give a gift is to acknowledge a facticity of preexistent goods and values, antedating their distribution in the artificially constructed private and public spheres. In the throes of such an acknowledgment, we can then ask with Alan Schrift, as he elaborates the logic of the gift in its drive to an ethic of generosity: "Might we then retrieve gift giving from the economic necessities imposed upon it within an exchangist economy and reframe the practices of giving in an account that does not restrict transactions to private proprietary relationships in which loans and loans paid back masquerade as the bestowal of gifts?"[33]

Hand in glove with a need for problematizing the sense of ownership in a market economy is the need to problematize the sense of owness in the philosophy of the subject as developed within modernity. It was modernity that was chiefly responsible for the concept of the self as isolated and enclosed, a zero-point consciousness that is somehow reflexively turned back upon itself, leading to a sharp demarcation of the edges between "mine" and "yours." In our shift to communicative praxis as textured by the transversal fibers of intersubjectivity, the distinction between mine and yours, although not obliterated, is denied its privileged status, calling for a reframing of the project of self-constitution.

Such a reframing requires a deconstruction of the modern, or Cartesian, platform for the "constitution of the subject"—a platform that proceeds from the invention of a monadic mind and an effort to locate self-identity in the depths of a recessed interiority. This Cartesian prejudice bequeathed to modernity the onerous task of marking out a path from one interiorized state of consciousness to another. Let us suppose, however, that these dichotomies and dualisms of "me" and "you," "mine" and "yours," are at best late arrivals in the adventure of selfhood. Let us further suppose that in the concrete history of the self in its quotidian social practices, no modern "problem of the existence of other minds" occurs. We then will be able to understand that, if we are indeed bent upon isolating philosophical "problems," there is more of a problem in determining the status of the "I" than that of the "we."

Against the backdrop of such a refiguration of subjectivity within the space of communicative intersubjectivity, the ontological weight of "my own," "your own," and what is "owed" by and to the both of us,

33. Schrift, *The Logic of the Gift*, 20.

is robustly attenuated. In turn, this points the way to a rescuing of the gift from the circle of debtor-creditor exchanges, freeing the ritual of giving a gift from incurring a debt that requires repayment. No longer a transaction of giving something that I "own," or a giving of "myself" as a collection of accumulated moral properties, mired in an economy of exchange relations, the giving of a gift is a practice that expects nothing in return. Indeed, it is unconditional. And *mutatus mutandis,* the receiving of a gift is an acknowledgment of the unconditionality in giving because there are no "commodities" to be exchanged.

This refiguration of subjectivity, with its deconstruction of the epistemological and the moral subject alike, makes all things new with regard to the so-called problem of presence. We are no longer searching for a self-identical "I" that strives to balance the account with another self-identical "I." Clearly there is still the other I/self/subject, that which Levinas names the third party, which calls both of us to justice. But this justice is no longer that of a distributive sort. Justice itself becomes transfigured and transvalued by dint of the presence of the gift. So we have a justice that is no longer simply symmetrical and reciprocal. It is now justice informed and vitalized by asymmetry, as is also the democracy, which is the socio-political expression of justice. Admittedly, this is a justice and a democracy that is yet to come. It has an eschatological orientation. It is that which we wait upon in our working. The gift of love as the asymmetrical dimension in all justice and democracy is the future as the possible. But the future as the possible is that which can be preenacted through a fitting response in the present of our communicative praxis as the moment that announces both the logos and the kairos.

A fitting response has its moment of origination in the incarnation of the logos in the voice and the face of the other. It is solicited by the incursion of exteriority rather than by the legislation of law within a recessed interiority. A fitting response finds its motivation in prior discourse, action, and the wider cultural contents that make up our historical inherence. The fitting response is always a response to that which is exterior and prior, and it is only through this responsiveness to that which is exterior and prior that ends, rights, duties, and goods come into play within the ethical economy. To be sure, ends, rights, duties, and goods remain the stuff of ethical action in civil society. But through the encounter with the gift, they become tempered by a depth dimension that was lacking before the possibility of an expenditure without return was disclosed.

The gift as the content and the measure of the fitting response is the depth dimension of the ethics of civil society, informing the preenactment of a justice and a democracy that is always yet to come. And it is this gift as unconditional alterity issuing a call to the inhabitants of a conditioned economy that comes to mind in the wake of our inquiries into a discourse of the God above God, God without Being, the religious without religion, and the call of conscience in the face of the neighbor.

Our journey began as a search for a grammar to enable us to talk and write about God in the present age. Throughout we have problematized discourses about the Deity that proceed from the usual spate of metaphysical and ontological categories. We have proposed instead a semantics of the gift, otherwise than being, without conditions, and beyond any expectations of return. Yet, in spite of its robust transcendence we have found that this gift can become efficacious within the economy of conditioned temporality, affording intimations of eternity within the folds of time. We began with the question about the meaning of God and we have ended up thinking and writing about the gift.

Works Cited

Aristotle. *Metaphysics*. In *The Basic Works of Aristotle,* edited by Richard McKeon. New York: Random House, 1941.

———. *Nicomachean Ethics*. In *The Basic Works of Aristotle,* edited by Richard McKeon. New York: Random House, 1941.

Augustine, Saint. *Concerning the City of God against the Pagans,* translated by Henry Scowcroft Bettensen. New York: Penguin Books, 1972.

Bataille, Georges. *The Accursed Share: An Essay on General Economy* Vol. 1. Translated by Robert Hurley. New York: Zone Books, 1989.

Bourdieu, Pierre. *The Logic of Practice*. Translated by Richard Nice. Cambridge, England: Polity Press, 1990.

Cadava, Eduardo, Peter Conner, Jean-Luc Nancy, editors. *Who Comes after the Subject?* New York: Routledge, 1991.

Cavell, Stanley. *The Claim of Reason: Wittgenstein, Skepticism, Morality, and Tragedy*. New York: Oxford University Press, 1979.

Casey, Edward S. *Getting Back into Place: Toward a Renewed Understanding of the Place-World*. Bloomington: Indiana University Press, 1993.

———. *The Fate of Place: A Philosophical History*. Berkeley: University of California Press, 1997.

Cooper, David A. *God Is a Verb: Kabbalah and the Practice of Mystical Judaism*. New York: Riverhead Books, 1997.

Deleuze, Gilles, and Félix Guattari. *A Thousand Plateaus: Capitalism and Schizophrenia*. Translated by Brian Massumi. Minneapolis: University of Minnesota Press, 1987.

Derrida, Jacques. "How to Avoid Speaking: Denials." In *Derrida and Negative Theology,* edited by Harold Coward and Toby Foshay. Albany: State University of New York Press, 1992.

———. "The Ends of Man." In *Margins of Philosophy,* translated by Alan Bass. Chicago: University of Chicago Press, 1982.

———. *The Gift of Death*. Translated by David Wills. Chicago: University of Chicago Press, 1995.

———. *The Politics of Friendship*. Translated by George Collins. New York: Verso Press, 1997.

Derrida, Jacques and Gianni Vattimo, editors. *Religion*. Stanford, Calif.: Stanford University Press, 1998.

Descartes, René. *Discourse on Method and Meditations*. Translated by Laurence J. Lafleur. New York: Liberal Arts Press, 1960.

Encyclopedia of Philosophy. Vol. 8. Editor in chief, Paul Edwards. New York: Macmillan, 1967.

Foucault, Michel. *The Order of Things: An Archaeology of the Human Sciences.* New York: Vintage Books, 1973.

———. "The Ethic of Care for the Self as a Practice of Freedom." In *The Final Foucault,* edited by James Bernauer and David Rasmussen. Cambridge, Mass.: MIT Press, 1988.

Freud, Sigmund. *The Future of an Illusion.* Translated by W. D. Robson-Scott. New York: H. Liveright, 1953.

Gadamer, Hans-Georg. *Reason in the Age of Science.* Translated by Frederick G. Lawrence. Cambridge, Mass.: MIT Press, 1984.

Habermas, Jürgen. *The Philosophical Discourse of Modernity: Twelve Lectures.* Trans. Frederick G. Lawrence. Cambridge: MIT Press, 1987.

Hallie, Philip P. *Lest Innocent Blood Be Shed: The Story of the Village of Le Chambon and How Goodness Happened There.* New York: Harper and Row, 1979.

Hegel, G. W. F. *Phänomenologie des Geistes.* Philosophische Bibliothek, sechste Auflage. Hamburg: Verlag von Felix Meiner, 1952.

Heidegger, Martin. "Appendix: Conversation with Martin Heidegger, Recorded by Hermann Noack." In *The Piety of Thinking,* translation, notes, and commentary by James. G. Hart and John C. Maraldo. Bloomington: Indiana University Press, 1976.

———. *Being and Time.* Translated by John Macquarrie and Edward Robinson. New York: Harper and Row, 1962.

———. *Der Satz vom Grund.* Tübingen, Germany: Günther Neske Pfullingen, 1958.

———. *Holzwege.* Frankfurt am Main: Vittorio Klostermann, 1950.

———. *Identity and Difference.* Translated by Joan Stambaugh. New York: Harper and Row, 1969.

———. *Kant and the Problem of Metaphysics.* Translated by James S. Churchill. Bloomington: Indiana University Press, 1962.

———. "Letter on Humanism." In *Martin Heidegger: Basic Writings,* rev. ed., edited by David Krell. San Francisco: HarperSanFrancisco, 1993.

———. "Phenomenology and Theology." In *The Piety of Thinking,* translation, notes, and commentary by James. G. Hart and John C. Maraldo. Bloomington: Indiana University Press, 1976.

———. "The Way Back into the Ground of Metaphysics." In *Existentialism from Dostoevsky to Sartre,* edited by Walter Kaufmann. New York: Meridian Books, 1956.

———. *Zur Seinsfrage.* Frankfurt: Vittoria Klosterman, 1956.

Hume, David. *Enquiries Concerning the Human Understanding and Concerning the Principles of Morals.* Edited by L. A. Selby-Bigge. Oxford, England: Clarendon Press, 1902.

Huntington, Patricia. *Ecstatic Subjects, Utopia, and Recognition: Kristeva, Heidegger, Irigaray.* Albany: State University of New York Press, 1998.

Husserl, Edmund. *Cartesian Meditations: An Introduction to Phenomenology.* Translated by Dorion Cairns. The Hague: M. Nijhoff, 1960.

———. *Die Krisis der europäischen Wissenschaften und die transzendentale Phänomenologie.* Edited by Walter Biemel. The Hague: M. Nijhoff, 1954.

Hyde, Michael J. *The Call of Conscience: Heidegger and Levinas, Rhetoric and the Euthanasia Debate.* Columbia: University of South Carolina Press, 2001.

———. "Rhetorically Man Dwells: On the Making-known Function of Discourse." *Communication* 7, 1983.

Johnson, Mark. *Moral Imagination: Implications of Cognitive Science for Ethics.* Chicago: University of Chicago Press, 1993.

Kant, Immanuel. *The Critique of Pure Reason.* Translated by Norman Kemp Smith. London: Macmillan, 1953.

Kegley, Charles W. and Robert Bretall, editors. *The Theology of Paul Tillich.* New York: Macmillan, 1952.

Kierkegaard, Søren. *Attack upon "Christendom," 1854–1855.* Translated by Walter Lowrie. Boston: Beacon Press, 1956.

———. *Concluding Unscientific Postscript.* Translated by David F. Swenson. Introduction and notes by Walter Lowrie. Princeton, N.J.: Princeton University Press, 1941.

———. *Either/Or: A Fragment of Life.* Vol. 2. Translated by Walter Lowrie. Princeton, N.J.: Princeton University Press, 1949.

———. *Philosophical Fragments or a Fragment of Philosophy.* Translated by David F. Swenson. Princeton, N.J.: Princeton University Press, 1936.

———. *Works of Love.* Edited and translated by Howard V. Hong and Edna H. Hong. Princeton, N.J.: Princeton University Press, 1995.

Kristeva, Julia. *Revolution in Poetic Language.* Translated by Margaret Waller. New York: Columbia University Press, 1984.

Lacan, Jacques. *The Language of the Self: The Function of Language in Psychoanalysis.* Translation by Anthony Wilden. Baltimore, Md.: Johns Hopkins University Press, 1968.

Levinas, Emmanuel. *Collected Philosophical Papers.* Translated by Alphonso Lingis. Boston: M. Nijhoff, 1987.

———. *Ethics and Infinity.* Translated by Richard A. Cohen. Pittsburgh: Duquesne University Press, 1985.

———. *Of God Who Comes to Mind.* Translated by Bettina Bergo. Stanford, Calif.: Stanford University Press, 1998.

———. *Otherwise than Being: or Beyond Essence.* Translated by Alphonso Lingis. Boston: M. Nijhoff, 1987.

———. *Time and the Other and Additional Essays.* Translated by Richard A. Cohen. Pittsburgh: Duquesne University Press, 1987.

———. "The Trace of the Other." In *Deconstruction in Context: Literature and Philosophy,* edited by Mark C. Taylor. Chicago: University of Chicago Press, 1986.

Lévi-Strauss, Claude. *The Savage Mind.* Chicago: University of Chicago Press, 1966.

Lyotard, Jean-François. *The Postmodern Condition: A Report on Knowledge.* Translated by Geoff Bennington and Brian Massumi. Minneapolis: University of Minnesota Press, 1984.

Macksey, Richard and Eugenio Donato. *The Languages of Criticism and the Sciences of Man: The Structuralist Controversy.* Baltimore, Md.: Johns Hopkins University Press, 1970.

Madison, Gary B. *The Political Economy of Civil Society and Human Rights.* New York: Routledge, 1998.

Marion, Jean-Luc. *God without Being: Hors-texte.* Translated by Thomas A. Carlson. Chicago: University of Chicago Press, 1991.

Miller, James. *The Passion of Michel Foucault.* New York: Simon and Schuster, 1993.

Mauss, Marcel. *The Gift: The Form and Reason for Exchange in Archaic Societies.* Trans. W. D. Halls. New York: W. W. Norton, 1990.

Nietzsche, Friedrich. *Beyond Good and Evil.* Translated by Marianne Cowan. Chicago: Gateway Editions, 1955.

———. *The Birth of Tragedy and the Case of Wagner.* Translated with commentary by Walter Kaufmann. New York: Vintage Books, 1967.

———. *The Birth of Tragedy and the Genealogy of Morals.* Translated by Francis Golffing. Garden City, N.Y.: Doubleday, 1956.

———. *Philosophy in the Tragic Age of the Greeks.* Translated by Marianne Cowan. Chicago: Henry Regnery, 1962.

———. *The Will to Power.* New translation by Walter Kaufmann and R. J. Hollingdale. Edited with commentary by Walter Kaufmann. New York: Random House, 1967.

———. *The Antichrist.* In *The Portable Nietzsche,* translated and edited by Walter Kaufmann. New York: Viking Press, 1954.

———. *The Gay Science.* In *The Portable Nietzsche,* translated and edited by Walter Kaufmann. New York: Viking Press, 1954.

———. *Thus Spake Zarathustra.* In *The Portable Nietzsche,* translated and edited by Walter Kaufmann. New York: Viking Press, 1954.

Plato. *Sophist.* In *The Dialogues of Plato.* Vol. 2. Translated by B. Jowett. New York: Random House, 1937.

———. *The Republic.* In *The Dialogues of Plato,* Vol. 1. Translated by B. Jowett. New York: Random House, 1937.

———. *Timaeus.* In *The Dialogues of Plato.* Vol. 2. Translated by B. Jowett. New York: Random House, 1937.

Polkinghorne, Donald. *Narrative Knowing and the Human Sciences.* Albany: State University of New York Press, 1988.

Ramsey, Ian T. *Religious Language: An Empirical Placing of Theological Phrases.* New York: Macmillan, 1963.

Ramsey, Ramsey Eric. *The Long Path to Nearness: A Contribution to a Corporeal Philosophy of Communication and the Groundwork for an Ethics of Relief.* Atlantic Highlands, N.J.: Humanities Press, 1998.

———. "Communication and Eschatology: The Work of Waiting, an Ethics of Relief, and Areligious Religiosity." *Communication Theory* 7:4 (1997), 343–61.

Ricoeur, Paul. *Oneself as Another.* Trans. Kathleen Blamey. Chicago: University of Chicago Press, 1992.

———. *Time and Narrative.* Vols. 1 and 2. Translated by Kathleen McLaughlin and David Pellauer; Vol. 3. Translated by Kathleen Blamey and David Pellauer. Chicago: University of Chicago Press, 1985–88.

Rorty, Richard. *Philosophy and the Mirror of Nature.* Princeton, N.J.: Princeton University Press, 1979.

Sartre, Jean-Paul. *Being and Nothingness: An Essay on Phenomenological Ontology.* Translated by Hazel E. Barnes. New York: Philosophical Library, 1956.

Schrag, Calvin O. *Communicative Praxis and the Space of Subjectivity.* Bloomington: Indiana University Press, 1986.

———. *Existence and Freedom: Towards an Ontology of Human Finitude.* Evanston: Northwestern University Press, 1961.

———. *The Resources of Rationality: A Response to the Postmodern Challenge.* Bloomington: Indiana University Press, 1992.

———. *The Self after Postmodernity.* New Haven, Conn.: Yale University Press, 1997.

———. "The Three Heideggers." In *Philosophical Papers: Betwixt and Between.* Albany: State University of New York Press, 1994.

Schrift, Alan D, editor. *The Logic of the Gift: Toward an Ethic of Generosity.* New York: Routledge, 1997.

Spinoza. "Ethics." In *Spinoza Selections,* edited by John Wild. The Modern Students Library. New York: Charles Scribner's Sons, 1930.

Tillich, Paul. *Dynamics of Faith.* New York: Harper, 1958.

———. *Systematic Theology.* Vol. 1. Chicago: University of Chicago Press, 1951.

———. *The Courage to Be.* New Haven, Conn.: Yale University Press, 1952.

van Huyssteen, J. Wentzel. "Is There a Postmodern Challenge in Theology and Science?" In *Essays in Postfoundationalist Theology.* Grand Rapids, Mich.: W. B. Eerdmans, 1997.

———. *The Shaping of Rationality: Toward Interdisciplinarity in Theology and Science.* Grand Rapids, Mich.: W. B. Eerdmans, 1999.

Walzer, Michael. *Spheres of Justice: A Defense of Pluralism and Equality.* New York: Basic Books, 1983.

Webb, Stephen H. *The Gifting God: A Trinitarian Ethics of Excess.* New York: Oxford University Press, 1996.

Young, Iris Marion. "Asymmetrical Reciprocity: On Moral Respect, Wonder, and Enlarged Thought." *Constellations: An International Journal of Critical and Democratic Theory* 3 (1997), 340–63.

Name Index

Subject Index

acknowledgment, 117–19, 139; gift of, 139, 139n; hermeneutics of, 117, 119–20

actuality: and possibility, 137; and potentiality, 8, 9, 85; pure, 9, 10

aesthetical, 49, 101–03, and ethical, 102–03; existence-spheres, 86, 101, 122; consciousness, 101, 112

aestheticism, 101, 102, 105

agapē, 111, 116, 120, 132

aletheia, 29

alterity, 64–65, 79–80, 96, 97, 101, 134–35

Anabaptist, 84

analogy, 16, 21; doctrine of, 15–16

anthropomorphism, 13, 53, 54

antichrist, 45, 93

antinomies, 21

Anwesenheit, 77

anxiety, 56–57, 124

apocalypticism, 25

a priori/a posteriori, 18

arborescent, 38, 52

aristocracy, 130

art, 49, 105; as culture-sphere, 37–38, 41

asymmetrical reciprocity, 126–27

atheology, 30; negative, 47

attestation, 117, 120

authenticity, 28

bad faith, 55

being: and becoming, 58; -for-itself and in-itself, 56–56, 66; great chain of, 10, 68; qua being, 8

Being: and beings, 9–10, 27, 67; erasure of, 27, 30, 69, 70, 78, 125; house of, 29, 72, 125; meaning of, 8, 27, 68, 77, 125; necessary, 6, 71; truth of, 16, 27, 30, 68, 77, 78, 125

capitalism, 36

caritas, 111, 132

Catholicism, 84, 88, 92

cause, 7, 8, 36; efficient, 6, 10; errant, 62; final, 6; infinite, 67

causa sui, 27, 28, 36, 56, 57, 67, 77

Chalcedon, Council of, 116

Christianity, 11, 35, 62, 84, 91, 93, 112, 116, 117, 130; cultural, 46; institutionalized, 45–46, 47; Platonized, 55

Christology, 116

cogito, 65, 77, 79, 81, 94

communicative praxis, 88, 121n, 142

communitarian, 98

conscience, 117, 124, 139

consciousness, 77, 79–80, 81, 94; historical, 135

cosmological: argument, 17; time, 42–43

Creator, 36, 67

criteria, 17–18, 24–25; verificationist, 18

culture-spheres, 37–38, 41, 122, 128

Dasein, 28, 29, 67, 122–24, 125; hermeneutics of, 28